# RAISING
# DEPRESSION-FREE
# CHILDREN

# RAISING DEPRESSION-FREE CHILDREN

*A Parent's Guide to Prevention and Early Intervention*

### KATHLEEN PANULA HOCKEY

 HAZELDEN®

Hazelden
Center City, Minnesota 55012-0176

1-800-328-0094
1-651-213-4590 (Fax)
www.hazelden.org

Library of Congress Cataloging-in-Publication Data
Hockey, Kathleen Panula.
    Raising depression-free children : a parent's guide to prevention and early
intervention / Kathleen Panula Hockey.
        p.   cm.
    Includes bibliographical references and index.
    ISBN 1-59285-042-1
    1. Depression in children.   2. Depression in children—Prevention.
3. Children—Mental health.   4. Stress in children—Prevention.   I. Title.

RJ506.D4H63 2003
618.92'8527—dc21

                                                                2003050830

07 06 05 04 03      6 5 4 3 2 1

Cover design by David Spohn
Interior design by Stanton Publication Services, Inc.
Typesetting by Stanton Publication Services, Inc.

The following publishers and individuals have generously given permission to use quo-
tations and adaptations from copyrighted works and workshops: excerpt from "Let the
Children Play," by Ellen Ruppel Shell, is reprinted with permission by *Hope Magazine*
(July/August 1998), www.hopemag.com; the "A, B, C's of Interpretation" are
reprinted with permission of Albert Ellis, Ph.D., and the Albert Ellis Institute; adapta-
tions from *Mind Over Mood: Change How You Feel by Changing the Way You Think,* by Dennis
Greenberger, Ph.D., and Christine A. Padesky, Ph.D., are printed with permission of
Guilford Press; adaptations from "Critical Thinking Skills" presented in a workshop by
Michael D. Yapko, Ph.D., are printed with permission of Dr. Yapko; adaptations from
*The Optimistic Child: A Proven Program to Safeguard Children against Depression and Build
Lifelong Resilience,* copyright ©1995, by Martin E. P. Seligman, Ph.D., Karen Reivich,
Ph.D., Lisa Jaycox, Ph.D., and Jane Gillham, Ph.D., are printed with permission of
Houghton Mifflin Company, all rights reserved.

*To my husband, Ron*

*and*

*to Andrew and Peter,*
*our two gifts from heaven*

# DISCLAIMER

Clinical depression is a complex medical condition that manifests itself in many forms. Using the techniques taught or the resources provided in this book do *not* guarantee that a particular adult, child, or adolescent can avoid the experience of clinical depression.

If you suspect that someone you know is suffering from clinical depression, contact a licensed medical or mental health professional in your area in order to ensure proper evaluation, diagnosis, and treatment. Listings of organizations that may be of assistance in locating a licensed professional are located in the back of this book.

A portion of the author's royalties from the sale of this book is being donated to the cause of preventing childhood depression.

# CONTENTS

# ACKNOWLEDGMENTS

This book is the fruit of a long personal and professional journey. Along the way, many people have inspired, supported, and assisted in its inspiration, creation, and completion. My heartfelt thanks to the following:

My parents, George Panula and Gwendolyn Burrows Panula, who—from hand-washing and "reality testing" commentaries of 1960s television shows to the early detection of life-threatening cancers—have practiced what is now preached in brochures across the country. They were preventionists even before the word *prevention* became part of the language. Happy forty-fifth wedding anniversary!

My husband, Ronald Hockey, the eternal optimist, whose companionship and help throughout the compositions, rejections, rewrites, and deadlines made the journey easier. A terrific dad, Ron often naturally modeled what I only wrote about and aspired to practice. We have been married sixteen wonderful years. I look forward to eighty more!

Our children, Andrew and Peter Hockey, who continue to teach me everything there is to know about being a parent. Providing never a dull moment, they actively participate in all our household adventures. During this adventure, they willingly went to after-school day care, took long bus rides home from school, and did extra chores so I could have more time to write. Their hugs, jokes, smiles, and constant surprises make home a welcome place after a hard day.

Michael D. Yapko, Ph.D., my teacher and mentor, whose work in the area of depression treatment and hypnosis formed the cornerstone on which my own work is built. His influence, personal and professional, is seen throughout this book. The use of activities and chapter summaries were inspired by his use of them in *Breaking the Patterns of Depression*.

Glee Palmer-Davis, L.I.C.S.W., executive director of the National Association of Social Workers, Washington State Chapter, who gave this unknown her first opportunity to present professional workshops on the topic of preventing childhood depression.

Sara Ellingson, L.I.C.S.W., a local colleague, who attended the first professional workshop and then suggested that this unknown transform the workshop into a book.

Hazelden, who agreed to publish this book when other publishers rejected it on the grounds that depression prevention wasn't marketable.

Rebecca Post, my editor at Hazelden, who remained ever enthusiastic and complimentary about this work. In addition to guiding me around potential pitfalls, she was like balm whenever self-doubt crept in. She made writing my first book a most enjoyable experience.

Kathryn Kjorlien, my manuscript editor, who dotted every *i*, crossed every *t*, and magnificently came up with just the right phrases when wording was a problem.

Terry Kneblik, a friend, who word processed large volumes of my handwritten scribble and then scribbled on the typed version where professional jargon needed to be removed for the "regular person." Her availability in a pinch and consistent hard work enabled me to finish the manuscript early.

Ron King, M.Ed., a colleague who, whenever I felt stressed or discouraged, lifted my spirits, made me laugh, and helped me put this project into "existential" perspective.

My colleagues and friends who provided thoughtful feedback on earlier versions of this book: Daniel Dye, M.D., Frances Dernbach, M.D., James Leedy, M.D., Sonja Hansen, R.N., Dan Lowe, Ph.D., Tae-Im Moon, Ph.D., Kathleen King, L.I.C.S.W., Susan Wolf, M.Ed., Susan Smith, M.Ed., and Suzi Tucker. Several changes were made to the text because of their informative and insightful comments, and I am indebted to them for giving their time to this project.

The staff at the Richland Public Library, who cheerfully filled out more than a hundred interlibrary loan applications during the five years I researched this topic.

Published authors and presenters Martin E. P. Seligman, Ph.D., Christine Padesky, Ph.D., Judith Beck, Ph.D., and Barbara Coloroso, M.Ed., who have influenced me both personally and professionally even though I have never had the privilege of meeting them except through their books or workshops.

The courageous people I have been privileged to work with professionally or have associated with through church, school, and extracurricular activities. These people inspire, humble, and provide me great hope for the future of the world.

Finally, in memory of Father Richard A. Wuertz, who asked to be remembered here only as a Catholic priest and a real human being. Father Wuertz hated any form of pretense and was himself as genuine as they come—whether people liked it or not. Inspired by his example, I have attempted to create a real book.

# INTRODUCTION

## BECOMING A PREVENTION PARENT

Confidence is what you have before you understand the situation.

—AUTHOR UNKNOWN

I was a smug therapist. My specialty was in the psychological treatment of children and families. For years I believed that because I had attended the better universities and had been trained by the "best of the best" in my field, I was an excellent therapist.

Then, I had my own children.

I probably would have remained arrogant even after having children, but for the fact that my firstborn suffered chronic medical problems that deprived him, my husband, and me of sleep for several years. Meanwhile, my second became the classic active child who made the notions of time to oneself and napping obsolete. We lived far from extended family and were too financially stretched to frequently hire baby-sitters. Consequently, in a few short years, the dynamic duo successfully exhausted me and conquered any semblance of self-confidence I might have thought I had. Eventually, I cowered in the face of frequent pitiful looks from parents of calm, compliant, and healthy children. Worse, I now received often-unsolicited advice about how to care for or parent my children so that they would be healthier or better behaved. So much for being a child and family specialist.

Suffice it to say, it didn't take long for this parent to join the ranks of the depressed. And although I didn't know it then, I was in good company. One out of every ten men and one out of every five women experience some form of depression during their lifetime.[1]

Eventually I recovered. My children, now school-aged, lead active lives and are a joy to behold, even if I still get occasional looks from other parents who wonder about my parenting skills. My oldest still has some chronic medical conditions that occasionally create difficulty but no longer interfere with his life. My youngest is still quite active, keeping my husband and me ever on our toes.

The story would have ended there except for the fact that I do not want my children to suffer my fate. It is widely known in professional circles that depression runs in families. Consequently, I have spent several years combing the literature on adult depression and childhood depression looking for concrete depression-preventing strategies. I was looking for something other than the usual "love your children" or "listen to your children." What I have found is both frightening and encouraging.

What is frightening is that childhood depression is on the rise. In fact, the rate of childhood depression is increasing faster than the rate of adult depression. And depressed children have a 40 to 60 percent chance of experiencing adult depression, compared to a 27 percent chance in nondepressed children.[2] Further, if a parent is depressed, his or her child—whether depressed or not—has a 40 to 70 percent chance of experiencing clinical depression or other major problems, including anxiety, oppositional or conduct problems, and alcohol or drug use and dependency, by the time the child reaches adulthood.[3] The problem is so serious that the World Health Organization has predicted that by the year 2020, when today's children reach adulthood, depression will rank as the second leading cause of "lost years of healthy life"—behind only ischemic heart disease. In 1990, depression ranked fourth.[4] What is even more frightening is that, in spite of these harrowing predictions, there is very little emphasis on depression prevention. Most books and articles on childhood depression emphasize identification and treatment, not prevention.

There is also encouraging news. Evidence suggests that some depressions may be preventable.[5] The fact that a child is at risk for depression by being born into a family with a history of depression, being raised in poverty, or having health problems doesn't mean that child is destined to become depressed. Notable researchers, including Martin E. P. Seligman, Ph.D., William Beardslee, M.D., and Tiffany Field, Ph.D., have documented the reality of depression prevention. I will summarize their research in chapter 3. In addition, research on resilience and strengths has inspired the introduction of resiliency parenting books and classes that fit with the notion of preventing depression in children.

If we are to reduce the anticipated number of depressed adults, we must begin with our children. They must be taught, from a very young age, how to live hopefully and optimistically even though the world can seem unpredictable and occasionally depressing. As you will see, depression is not solely a matter of genetics and biology. There are very specific things parents can do to help reduce their child's risk for depression or to reduce the risk of relapse if their child has already experienced the illness.

Some of the preventive interventions described in this book are based on the research-backed techniques of Martin E. P. Seligman, Ph.D., and his colleagues Karen Reivich, Ph.D., Jane Gillham, Ph.D., and Lisa Jaycox, Ph.D. Others are drawn from the clinical works of Milton H. Erickson, M.D., Albert Ellis, Ph.D., Judith Beck, Ph.D., Christine Padesky, Ph.D., and Michael D. Yapko, Ph.D., whose contributions to the fields of psychology and depression treatment are widely known. I have also drawn information from the profuse literature on social skills training and parenting techniques, including the recent resiliency books and programs just mentioned. All of these sources are cited and listed in the bibliography.

The final source for this book is a not-so-smug-anymore therapist/parent who has learned that sometimes experience can be the best teacher. Along with the usual case vignettes that accompany books such as this, I have recorded some of my own failures and successes on the road to becoming a proactive, prevention parent. It is my hope that this blend of personal experience and professional know-how will inspire you to take action on behalf of your child.

You don't have to be a perfect parent to practice depression prevention and early intervention, nor do you have to wait for institutions and offices of public policy to create large-scale programs for your children. These programs are sorely needed but, unfortunately, are years away. You, as a parent, can begin *now*. You already have the ability to profoundly influence your child's emotional health. I invite you to join me in practicing the many realistic and practical ways to reduce your child's risk for depression. We owe it to our future and our children's future.

## HOW TO USE THIS BOOK

This book is designed for parents of infants to twelve-year-olds. It is divided into two parts. The first part provides basic information about the topic of childhood depression and prevention. It is written simply and will reference other books that provide more detailed information. The second part of the book, the "meat and potatoes," is about parenting strategies that can help reduce the risk for the onset or recurrence of childhood depression.

Throughout the book, you will find activities that are labeled "Something You Can Do." These are designed to provide you with specific tasks that can help you identify problems early and also promote resiliency in your children. Because I understand the stresses of parenthood, I can assure you that these activities are designed simply.

In addition, activities called "Something to Think About" are also sprinkled throughout the book. These are designed to help you clarify your thoughts, attitudes, and beliefs about depression-related topics. Passing on depression-resistant beliefs to children is as important as any skill learned.

All vignettes in the book describe concepts and correct skill-building techniques. As stated, some of the vignettes are actual events that have occurred in my own home. The rest are fictitious composites of people I have worked with in my counseling practice and people I have observed in parks, classrooms, and team-sport events. The names, genders, ages, and situational details have been changed to preserve the anonymity of those involved.

Finally, I use the pronouns *he* and *she* interchangeably at times, in an attempt to give each gender fair representation throughout the book.

# PART 1

===

# UNDERSTANDING CHILDHOOD
# DEPRESSION AND PREVENTION

# CHAPTER 1

---

# Is Your Child at Risk for Depression?

*I feel that I have set them up for a lifetime of depression.*

—IN "PRIMARY PREVENTION OF CHILDHOOD DEPRESSION:
BEYOND BIOLOGY," *SOCIAL WORK TODAY*

Michael, age ten, moved with his parents to a new city. In doing so, he left his friends, soccer teammates, and familiar school. Although at first he seemed to adjust well, soon his parents noticed that Michael had lost his usual sense of humor. He lost his appetite and his ability to concentrate on his homework. He also complained of having trouble sleeping.

A phone call to the school revealed a different picture. Michael seemed to be fitting in with his peers, was keeping up with his schoolwork, and even laughed on occasion. He had joined the school soccer team, and his coach was pleased with how he fit in with the rest of the team. Michael was often seen joking with his teammates.

When Michael's parents questioned him about his

sullen mood at home, Michael burst into tears and said, "I miss Bobby and Mitch. Why did we have to move?"

Later that night, an argument ensued between Michael's parents.

"I told you not to take this job! Michael isn't the type of kid that can handle change well."

"You can't stop life just because your son wants things to stay the same! The money is better here. In the long run, it will be better for all of us."

"But I'm worried about him. He's depressed. Depression runs on my side of the family, you know."

"What do you mean 'depressed'? He's doing just fine. His grades are good. He's playing soccer and making friends. He just needs a little time. If you just quit pampering him, he'll get over it!"

---

When is a child clinically depressed? When is he at risk for depression? When is he simply going through a phase? These are difficult questions to answer.

Popular magazines, news articles, television stories, and advertisements all tend to highlight the biological aspects of depression and depression treatment. This can influence some parents to dismiss their child's depressive symptoms as a phase simply because they don't want to believe their child could have the disease of depression. Conversely, other parents may interpret their child's every negative feeling as a sign of clinical depression because they believe their child has inherited a genetically transmitted condition that needs to be medicated or cured.

In real life, neither of these positions is a good one. Childhood depression, a medical illness, has *many* influencing factors, both genetic and environmental, that become risk factors when they affect a particular child.

When we observe our children, we need to think through all the potential influences and risk factors. Jumping to conclusions about our children's emotional health because of our unfounded beliefs does not help our children. In the previous vignette, for example, there is simply not enough information presented to determine whether Michael is clinically depressed or simply grieving the loss of his friends. A more thorough professional assessment would need to be made, especially if Michael's symptoms persisted.

### BELIEFS THAT CHANGE

Before you continue, take a few minutes to record your answers to the questions in "Something to Think About #1." They are designed to help you become aware of your beliefs about depression.

---

### Something to Think About #1
#### *Your Beliefs about Depression*

What are your beliefs about childhood depression? Is it a biological disease, psychological problem, or fad created by professionals? What do you think causes childhood depression? Bad parenting? Genes? Chemical imbalance? Evil?

Who helped shape your beliefs? Advertisements? Family physician or therapist? Church minister? Articles in popular magazines? Books?

How have your beliefs influenced how you have or have not addressed the issue of depression prevention with your child?

---

Our beliefs shape our attitudes and approaches to problems. While reading this chapter, keep in mind your beliefs and compare them with the facts I will present here. Perhaps you may choose to reconsider your beliefs.

## THE MANY FACTORS

There are three areas of research in the study of depression: biology, psychology, and sociology. The biological area examines the influence of genes, heredity, hormones, and the complex chemical processes of the brain. The psychological area examines coping styles, thought processes (how one thinks about life events), parent-child interactions, and the effects of life experiences on thought processes. Finally, the sociological area compiles statistics that demonstrate the influence of factors such as socioeconomic status (poverty versus wealth), cultural values and beliefs, technology, and the mass media. Often, researchers cross these lines of separation in order to provide combined information. Examples of this are the effects of trauma or stress (psychology) on brain chemistry (biology), the effects of poverty (sociology) on thought processes (psychology), and the effects of corrective psychotherapies (psychology) on brain function (biology).

Let us examine these areas in more detail. While doing so, begin to consider which areas might be risk factors for your child. Later in this chapter, I will provide a summary list of risk factors and explain how to interpret that list when evaluating your child.

## Biology
### Heredity
Studies of identical twins raised apart and studies of adopted children with depressed biological parents provide some in-

formation about how much of childhood depression is inherited. According to a 2001 report published by Harvard Health Publications, the genetic components of depression are hard to pin down. However, there is evidence that a person who has a first-degree relative (mother, father, sister, or brother) with clinical depression has a 1.5 to 3 percent higher than normal risk of experiencing clinical depression. Even within the scope of these statistics, investigators have found it difficult to sort out the actual influence of genes versus learned behavior or other situational factors.[1]

*Chemical Imbalances in the Brain*
Today, brain imaging techniques such as positron-emission tomography (PET) and functional magnetic resonance imaging (fMRI) have allowed scientists to study the brain much more closely than in the past. Through these studies, we know that the parts of the brain related to emotion become activated or shut down to a greater degree when a person becomes clinically depressed. These states sometimes remain even after a person recovers from an episode of clinical depression. We also know that the brain's chemical-electrical processes, which allow messages to be sent from one part of the brain to another, become impaired when a person is clinically depressed.[2] These are the reasons why, once a diagnosis of clinical depression is made, a physician may prescribe an antidepressant medication. Medication can correct the chemical-electrical impairments and reduce the over- or underactivity of the emotional centers of the brain.

*Hormones*
Scientists believe there may be a relationship between hormones and clinical depression, but so far, the nature of that relationship is unclear. We do know that in childhood, boys

and girls have about the same rates of clinical depression. However, at the onset of puberty, the rate for girls is higher than the rate for boys. We also know that women can suffer from what is commonly called premenstrual syndrome and postpartum depression—both of which men do not experience. For these reasons, "being female" is often found on the list of risk factors for depression.[3]

*Medical Conditions and Medication Side Effects*
In his book *You Can Beat Depression,* John Preston, Psy.D., lists twenty-six medical diseases and disorders that can cause depressive symptoms. He also lists twenty-one pharmaceutical medications that can cause side effects of depressive symptoms. This is why an assessment for depression often includes a medical history and evaluation. In children, what looks like clinical depression may actually be thyroid or neurological problems, vitamin deficiencies, endocrine disorders, sleep disorders, severe allergies, diseases of the immune system, or viruses such as the flu or mononucleosis. In some children, even prolonged antibiotic use can create side effects of mild to moderate depressive symptoms. It is important to remember that depressive symptoms are *not* the disease of depression. The latter is much more complex.

*Genes*
To date, no specific gene or group of genes has been clearly identified as a cause of clinical depression. When a gene or gene group for depression is identified, it will still not be implicated as the cause of depression. Gene research has demonstrated quite clearly that, with the exception of eye color and some other physical attributes, genetic influence is not necessarily destiny. Rather, a *genetic-environmental interplay* deter-

mines whether a specific gene vulnerability evolves into a particular trait or disease.[4]

---

**Something You Can Do #1**
*Your Child's Medical History*

Make a list of your child's medical history beginning with any unusual events during pregnancy (such things might include physical trauma to the mother, accidents, death of a loved one during pregnancy, medications taken during pregnancy, and maternal depression). In your child's early years, did she have surgery, major illnesses, medical conditions, or allergies, or did she take regular medications?

Make a list of this child's biological family medical history. Did a biological parent or grandparent suffer from thyroid problems, allergies, cancer, asthma, diabetes, and so on? Was this parent or grandparent on regular medication, especially when he or she was a child?

Keep this information on file so that if your child develops depressive symptoms, you can help a physician rule out other medical problems.

---

## Psychology

*Prolonged Stress*

Scientists have discovered that prolonged stress can actually cause changes in brain chemistry and structure very similar to the changes noted in clinically depressed individuals.[5] It is also known that there is a statistically higher incidence of childhood depression with certain types of stresses. Some of these are chronic medical problems, a history of child abuse or molestation, living in a family that frequently argues and fights, and living with an alcoholic or drug-abusing parent.[6]

*Losses*

Loss or bereavement is a unique type of stress. Loss of a parent or sibling through death is an obvious traumatic loss. Divorce or separation, family relocation, or having parents who are too preoccupied to be emotionally available are not as obvious. They are, however, still considered losses and, therefore, potentially contributing factors in the development of childhood depression. Studies also indicate a significant relationship between childhood depression and "latchkey" children, children of alcoholics, and children of parents with a mental health diagnosis.[7]

*Coping Styles and Thought Processes*

Research has demonstrated a significant relationship between childhood depression and negative thought patterns, called pessimism. Other significant links are the inability to solve problems, poor social skills, and a lack of a stable value system. These create low self-esteem and poor coping styles that fail when adversity strikes. Pessimism, low self-esteem, and poor coping skills taken together are sure to create a sense of helplessness and hopelessness, the psychological hallmarks of clinical depression.[8]

*Coexisting Conditions*

For reasons yet unknown, childhood depression often co-exists with other mental health diagnoses. Included are attention deficit disorder (inattentive or hyperactive type), obsessive-compulsive disorder, oppositional defiant disorder, conduct disorder, and anxiety disorders. Anxiety disorders, in fact, often precede childhood depression.[9] Such coexistence with its overlapping symptoms makes diagnosing childhood depression difficult even for the most seasoned professional.

---

### Something You Can Do #2
#### *Your Child's Mental Health History*

Make a list of your child's mental health history, if any. Has your child been diagnosed with anxiety, depression, attention deficit disorder, or something else? Also include things like past counseling experiences, hospitalizations, or medications.

Then make a list of your child's family mental health history. Include parents, stepparents, grandparents, and whoever else might have been a live-in caretaker for your child. Is there a family history of depression, alcoholism, attention deficit disorder, sleep disorders, or some other disorder? Did the biological mother suffer postpartum depression that lasted longer than two weeks? If so, were other caretakers involved with the infant?

In addition, list any losses or unusual stresses your child may have experienced recently and in the past. This list can include things like the death of a favorite pet, a difficult day care experience, major surgery, an accident, school pressures, and so on.

Finally, list any difficulties your child seems to have *repeatedly,* such as trouble making friends, low self-esteem, shyness, or impulsive behaviors.

The information you have outlined in this activity is helpful for professionals trying to make a diagnosis during an assessment. But more important, it gives you a place to target your own preventive interventions as you continue to read this book.

---

## Sociology

*Socioeconomic Class*

Estaban Cardemil, Ph.D., and his colleagues, in their 2002 paper "The Prevention of Depressive Symptoms in Low-Income Minority Middle School Students," report that "although the research is mixed with respect to minority status and depression, researchers have consistently noted high rates of depressive symptoms among low-income populations." He then cites a national survey on coexisting conditions, which found that the report of a pure depressive episode is 1.6 times greater for those individuals with an income of less than $20,000 per year than those with more than $70,000 per year.[10] Poverty can be a contributing factor in the development of childhood depression.

*Technology*

There is no doubt that the advances in technology since the 1940s is staggering. With these advances come certain societal values and expectations that can contribute to the development of childhood depression. Examples include information overload, the stress of having too many choices (Have you ever brought your young child into a grocery store?), and the ability to have instant gratification (Hungry? Don't wait. Just "drive through."). Data indicate that as a country becomes more technologically advanced, the rates of depression climb.[11]

*The Mass Media*

The influence of the mass media is not confined to the effect of watching too much television violence. Advertisements, music, and news reports can also shape our values and outlook on life. In the 1940s, we lived in an era of duty, God, and country. In the 1950s, we were in the era of "happy days."

During the 1970s, the "me generation" evolved. In the 19... we lived in the "culture of death" and the "age of melancholy." Then, the war on terrorism in 2001 suddenly heralded what some called a "new age of anxiety." Indeed, the average person is currently bombarded with anxiety-provoking media messages *daily*.

On a different note, scientists have also found neurological and developmental problems in young children who spend too much time in front of television. This is due to the *very nature of the medium* rather than any content viewed. Therefore, *all* media—computers, Nintendos, PlayStations, and other such devices—need to be considered. Problems include difficulties in relating to real-life situations, the absence of problem-solving skills, and an inability to form healthy peer relationships. Childhood depression is also associated with these same difficulties. The research in this area is so compelling that the American Academy of Pediatrics (AAP) recommends no more than one to two hours of television per day for children and *no* television for children under the age of two. In 2001, the AAP published a brochure on the topic that provides practical strategies and suggestions for parents to help offset the negatives of the mass media. Details are provided in "Something You Can Do #3."

In addition to these problems, children tend to absorb from the media a set of values and beliefs that can set them up for serious disappointments, which can lead to depression later in life. Some of these beliefs are

- I can have it all
- I can become anything I imagine
- I am entitled to whatever I want
- I can get even if someone prevents me from getting what I want

- it's okay to get what I want with force
- the more I have, the happier I will be
- I must be famous, glamorous, or rich to be somebody
- if I am unhappy, it is someone else's fault

In addition, girls are often influenced to believe they must be thin, sexy, and almost unrealistically attractive to be worthwhile people. Boys are influenced to believe they must be handsome, strong, tough yet sensitive, and successful.

These beliefs are acquired unconsciously, which makes them a very powerful influence. The difference between conscious learning and unconscious learning will be discussed in chapter 4. Meanwhile, parents need to be aware of the messages children are sometimes receiving through the mass media. Over time, these messages can shape a child's values, perceptions, and expectations about life if parents do not play an active role in building skills that counter them.

---

### Something You Can Do #3
#### *Browse Brochures*

Write or call the American Academy of Pediatrics. Ask for a copy of the brochure "Understanding the Impact of Media on Children and Teens." Browse the other brochures the AAP provides.

American Academy of Pediatrics
141 Northwest Point Boulevard
Elk Grove Village, IL 60007-1098
847-434-4000
www.aap.org

---

## RISK FACTORS

It is clear that the development of childhood depression is influenced by a number of different factors. This is why no one person or thing can be blamed for the illness if it does occur. For each child, a *unique* combination of influencing factors may, if left unaddressed, develop into clinical depression. This is why practicing depression prevention *at home* is so important.

Below is a summary of risk factors for childhood depression based on the influencing factors just discussed. Take a moment to think about your own family in light of these risk factors.

- having a prior clinical depressive episode
- having a depressed parent
- experiencing the death of a loved one
- having low-level depressive symptoms
- experiencing a recent major loss (such as parental divorce or change in location)
- having a family history of clinical depression or drug and alcohol abuse
- having a diagnosis of attention deficit disorder (inactive or hyperactive type), obsessive-compulsive disorder, oppositional defiant disorder, conduct disorder, or an anxiety disorder
- having a history of abuse or trauma
- having a history of chronic or serious medical problems
- living in a family that frequently fights or is violent
- living with acute or chronic stress in the environment
- habitually interpreting life events negatively (pessimism)

The number-one predictor of childhood depression is whether that child has already experienced clinical depression. The number-two predictor is whether a parent has experienced depression. All the other risk factors show varying degrees of influence in depression's development. The last risk factor, "habitually interpreting life events negatively," will be explained in detail in chapter 7.

If your child has one or more of these risk factors, it doesn't necessarily mean she will develop clinical depression. It means that her chances of developing it are greater than a child with no risk factors. It is also important to realize that no one risk factor puts a child at greater risk than the general population. There must be more than one risk factor. In other words, this list needs to be interpreted cumulatively. The more risk factors a child has, the more likely it is for that child to develop depression. There are many children who have experienced poverty, trauma, and chronic illnesses who have not developed depression. There are many offspring of depressed or alcoholic parents who do not become clinically depressed.

The notion of risk factors and being at risk for depression are important concepts from a prevention standpoint. Many risk factors are changeable. Depression prevention, therefore, begins with reducing the number of risk factors whenever possible. Take a moment to complete "Something You Can Do #4." This exercise will help you apply the risk-factor list to your own children.

Most children will be at risk for depression some time during the course of their development. Each stage of growing up brings new and different stresses that can challenge the mental health of even the most hardy of children. The more emotionally prepared the child, the better equipped he is to pass through each stage—even if serious adversity occurs.

---

### Something You Can Do #4
*List Risk Factors*

Make a list of each of your children's particular risk factors. Be specific. Different children in the same home may have different risk factors.

Keep the list handy as you continue to read this book so that you can match a protective skill with a risk factor.

If any risk factor involves your own history or problems between you and your spouse/significant other, take initial steps to solve these problems (see a doctor or therapist, go to couple's counseling, and so on). Removing even one risk factor from your child's personal list automatically reduces his or her risk for depression.

---

### SUMMARY

- Personal beliefs shape our attitudes and approaches to problems.
- There are three areas of depression study: biology, psychology, and sociology.
- Risk factors are the numerous influencing factors that contribute to the development of depression for a particular individual.
- There are more than twelve depression risk factors for children.
- Risk factors are assessed cumulatively.

# CHAPTER 2

## WHAT IS CHILDHOOD
## DEPRESSION, REALLY?

Depression is painful.

—JOHN PRESTON, *YOU CAN BEAT DEPRESSION*

### CHILDHOOD DEPRESSION

Thirty years ago, it was common belief that only the most "mentally disordered" children experienced depression. This perception changed some in the 1980s. However, the greatest theoretical shift occurred in the mid-1990s with advances in brain imaging technology. Suddenly, researchers could see changes in brain function among depressed individuals. Shortly thereafter, clinical depression became more commonly thought of as a medical disease rather than a condition of weak will. More specifically, it was defined as a brain disorder in which "the neural circuits responsible for the regulation of moods, thinking, sleep, appetite, and behavior fail to function properly."[1] Just like other diseases, such as diabetes or heart disease, depression has many different types and levels of severity. Just as *any* adult could experience depression, so could *any* child. The causes of depression are complex and unique for each child.

The National Institute of Mental Health estimates that 2.5 percent of all children and 8.3 percent of all adolescents will experience some form of clinical depression.[2] Some estimates suggest as many as *one in eleven* children may experience some form of clinical depression before the age of fourteen.[3]

The National Institute of Mental Health has also sponsored research indicating that without proper treatment, childhood depression tends to repeat throughout childhood and into adolescence and adulthood, with each successive episode becoming more severe.[4] Depression in children has also been linked to eventual cigarette smoking, substance abuse, academic difficulties, physical and health problems, and suicidal behaviors.[5] This is why intervention and relapse prevention is so important for children who have already experienced *even a mild* form of depression or exhibit depressive symptoms even though not diagnosed with clinical depression.

## SYMPTOMS OF CLINICAL DEPRESSION

To date, no specific set of clinical criteria exists that exclusively describes childhood depression. Clinicians rely on the criteria outlined for diagnosing adults found in the American Psychiatric Association's fourth edition of the *Diagnostic and Statistical Manual of Mental Disorders (DSM-IV)*.

The *DSM-IV* lists nine criteria for a major depressive episode. Simplified, they are

- feeling depressed, sad, or melancholy most of the day, nearly every day
- the inability to experience pleasure or excitement even when doing activities that used to be pleasurable

- serious weight loss or weight gain in a short period of time
- sleeping too much, too little, or not well
- sluggish or jittery movements that are noticed by other people
- feeling tired and experiencing low motivation or loss of energy nearly every day
- feeling guilty a lot, feeling worthless, feeling inadequate
- having trouble thinking clearly, being unable to concentrate or make decisions
- feeling helpless and hopeless, having thoughts of death or suicide or having a plan for suicide

An adult must have at least five of these nine symptoms during a two-week period in order to be diagnosed with major depression. The symptoms must also be preventing a person from functioning well in daily life.

The only comment found in the *DSM-IV* about children is that "in children the depressed mood can be an irritable mood."[6] In other words, a child may have angry outbursts or frequent temper tantrums.

David G. Fassler, M.D., and Lynne Dumas, in their book *"Help Me, I'm Sad,"* outline specific symptoms for diagnosing clinical depression in children according to age group, from infancy to adolescence. They list a total of forty-six symptoms of clinical depression for children. This illustrates the complexity of diagnosing childhood depression and the incompleteness of the *DSM-IV.*

If you are concerned that your child is clinically depressed, don't try to diagnose her yourself. Take her to her primary care physician and also a *licensed* mental health professional. Some organizations that can assist you in locating a physician or other professional are listed in the "Resources" section of this book.

### TYPES OF CLINICAL DEPRESSION

There are several types of clinical depression that describe specific conditions in children and adults. The criteria listed on pages 26–27 describe the symptoms of an episode of unipolar depression or the depressive phase of bipolar depression.

During an episode of unipolar depression, a person sinks low emotionally and feels stuck there. It takes great effort to accomplish even the smallest daily task. In a serious case, a person cannot motivate himself to get out of bed in the morning. Episodes of unipolar depression can occur one time or many times over a lifetime. Each episode can be mild, moderate, or severe.

People who experience bipolar depression also experience the depressive episodes just described. In addition, they experience manic or hypomanic episodes partially characterized by a decreased need for sleep, grandiosity, irritability, and very high energy. These manic or hypomanic episodes are not the typical ups and downs of moodiness. They are exaggerated so that others can clearly see something unusual. During a manic episode, a person with severe bipolar depression might go on spending sprees, commit many sexual transgressions, become violent, or buy airline tickets in order to run away from home. As with unipolar depression, a person with bipolar depression can suffer one or many depressive or manic episodes ranging from mild to severe.

It used to be believed that children could not experience bipolar depression. Recent observations and study have indicated otherwise. In their book *The Bipolar Child*, Demitri Papolos, M.D., and Janice Papolos describe in detail the signs, symptoms, and treatment for bipolar depression in children. Caution is still used, however, when assessing children for bipolar depression. In 2002, the *Harvard Mental Health Letter,* a publication of the Harvard Medical School, stated that full-blown bipolar depression in children is still considered uncommon.[7]

Dysthymia is a type of clinical depression that has similar symptoms as unipolar depression, but the symptoms are less intense and last a long time. In fact, a clinician cannot diagnose dysthymia in children unless the symptoms have existed for at least one year. A child suffering from dysthymia can go on to suffer an episode of unipolar or bipolar depression later in life.

Finally, there are two forms of clinical depression often diagnosed in children when the symptoms are mild but still meet the requirements for diagnosis. They are depression not otherwise specified (NOS) and adjustment disorder with depressed mood.

Depression NOS is diagnosed when a child has less than five of the nine symptoms for a depressive episode.

Adjustment disorder with depressed mood is diagnosed when there is an identifiable stressor that is obviously triggering the child's symptoms, but when the child's symptoms seem more serious than the situation warrants. Stressors can include a death in the family, divorce, relocation, or even a change in status, such as moving from grade school to middle school.

Even while all these classifications and more exist for clinical depression, it is important to realize that there are as many unique ways of manifesting the illness as there are children. In my practice, I have worked with children who are diagnosed with a clinical depressive episode whose most visible symptom was not sadness, but anger, withdrawal, or great difficulty concentrating. Children with depression exhibit more than one symptom, and sadness may not be the most prominent. Each child is unique.

Symptom lists are only meant as general guidelines. Knowing your child so that you can notice changes in your child's mood, thoughts, or behavior is a much better tool. In part 2 of this book, I provide exercises that will train you to become more observant of your child on a day-to-day basis. *One important aspect of depression prevention is early recognition of a child needing help.*

## CLINICAL DEPRESSION VERSUS NORMAL SADNESS

There is another consideration adding to the complexity of diagnosing clinical depression in children. Many depressions experienced by children are not clinical. We use the term *depressed* to mean sad, blue, melancholy, and even frustrated. Consider Brittany, a twelve-year-old who discovers a lone pimple on her chin. She telephones her friend Jessica and exclaims, "You wouldn't believe it! I got a zit! It's on my chin! Everyone will see! *I'm soooo depressed!*" Brittany then mopes and hides in her room for a while. She may be depressed, but she is not clinically depressed.

The symptoms for normal sadness and clinical depression can be the same. What usually differentiates the two is *how* those symptoms are manifested. In normal sadness, the symptoms of depression are mild, last a short time, and are experienced only in some areas of a child's life. In clinical depression, the symptoms are more serious, last a long time (two weeks or more), and are experienced in most or all areas of a child's life.

Remember that one guideline for diagnosing clinical depression is that *the symptoms must be present for two weeks or longer.* This is because people can react to stressful events with symptoms that mimic clinical depression. Who has acted happy and optimistic while experiencing the flu?

When professionals assess children for clinical depression, often they ask about the child's level of functioning at school, with friends, and at home. If the child is demonstrating impairments in all three areas, the clinician sees a red flag for clinical depression. Conversely, if a child is manifesting depressive symptoms only in one area, at home for example, the clinician might pursue the resolution of a situational problem before concluding the child is clinically depressed. As emphasized thus far, depression encompasses a wide range of feelings and behaviors.

## SIGNS AND SYMPTOMS OF DEPRESSION IN CHILDREN

Diagnosing children with clinical depression can be a difficult task for physicians and mental health professionals. Part of the process is to gather information from parents, teachers, and if possible, friends.

Below is a list of signs and symptoms of depression in children. It is a composite of many lists found in many childhood depression books. The list is divided into four categories: physical, emotional, cognitive (thinking style), and behavioral. Childhood depression may be experienced in one area or several.

Physical:
- significant weight loss or weight gain
- appetite changes: eating too much or too little food
- physical complaints: stomachaches, headaches, and so on

- sleeping too little, too much, or not well; frequent nightmares
- tired all the time; loss of energy; exhaustion

Emotional:
- depressed, sad, or tearful mood
- moodiness; mood swings; easily angered
- anxious, nervous, fearful; worries a lot
- feels guilty a lot; hates self
- feels helpless to change negative situations
- feels hopeless about the future
- seems overly sensitive to criticism or correction

Cognitive:
- thoughts of running away
- suicidal thoughts; thoughts of death or death-related themes
- self-defeating or self-hating thoughts
- helpless and hopeless thoughts
- mostly negative thoughts about most situations (pessimism)
- many thoughts that create excessive or irrational guilt

Behavioral:
- slipping grades
- loss of playfulness or zest for life
- easily discouraged or frustrated
- increased whininess or aggressiveness
- loss of interest in usual pleasurable activities or hobbies
- social isolation; withdrawal
- difficulty concentrating; can't make choices
- can't finish projects

- lets life happen rather than helping to shape its direction
- overactivity; restlessness
- quiet, monotone, one-word answers to questions
- developmentally "going backward," such as soiling pants at age six
- self-injurious behaviors, such as head-banging and cutting oneself
- talking, writing, singing, or drawing about death or suicide
- habitually listening to music with death- or suicide-related themes
- habitually reading books, reading comics, or playing videos with death- or suicide-related themes

Exhibiting a few of these does not necessarily mean your child has clinical depression. She may be experiencing normal sadness, other medical problems, a situational problem, or something else that indicates a different diagnosis or no diagnosis at all. That is why, if you have concerns, you should *not* attempt to diagnose your child yourself but instead get a more thorough assessment by a qualified professional. If your child is talking about death or suicide, it is *vital* that you seek professional help *immediately.*

As stated before, a good place to start the process of assessment is with your child's primary care physician. A physician can evaluate for any medical problems that might be causing depressive symptoms. (Page 14 of chapter 1 discusses several medical conditions that mimic depressive symptoms.) In addition, a primary care physician usually has a list of psychologists, psychiatrists, or licensed master's-degree-level therapists and can often facilitate a referral if needed.

If a thorough assessment by a physician and/or clinician

rules out clinical depression, it is not time to relax and go on with life as usual. *Depression prevention is needed.* From a prevention viewpoint, these signs and symptoms are also target areas for preventive interventions.

## THE PROBLEM OF HASTY DIAGNOSIS

An eight-year-old girl was referred to my office for clinical depression. Her symptoms were relatively mild. Before seeing me, her parents took her to her primary care physician. The physician asked a few questions during a fifteen-minute visit and, based on the answers, diagnosed the child with unipolar depression and prescribed an antidepressant. The parents did not object. Instead, they arrived at my office feeling guilty and fearful.

Most physicians are more careful before diagnosing and prescribing an antidepressant for a child. However, this kind of hasty diagnosing can and does occur. As stated before, clinical depression in children is a complex matter. It certainly should not be diagnosed in fifteen minutes. All other serious medical conditions are diagnosed only after the physician has ruled out simpler possibilities.

In contrast to the above example, consider the physician who suspects clinical depression but refers the child for lab work and assessment by a mental health specialist. The physician then sets up a follow-up appointment to consider antidepressant medication, after the lab test results are completed and she has had a chance to talk with the child's therapist about situational factors that may be causing the child's symptoms. This is a reasonable approach unless the child is seriously suicidal or speaking or acting bizarrely. In that case, the physician would immediately refer that child to a psychiatrist or psychiatric hospital. Thankfully, most physicians practice in this manner. In addition, some large managed care companies now require such a procedure from their primary care physicians.

Hasty diagnosing isn't confined to physicians. Psychologists, social workers, and other mental health professionals sometimes see depressive symptoms and jump to the conclusion that the child should immediately see a physician for medication even before beginning therapy.

Most experts in the field of child psychiatry and child psychology recommend a conservative approach when considering antidepressant medication for children. Very little research exists on the long-term effects of using these drugs with children. Tricyclic antidepressants, the "safe" standard fifteen years ago, have been found to cause heart problems and death in some children.[8] Although the sample in the actual study reporting this information was very small (seventy-five children), in 1999, the American Academy of Child and Adolescent Psychiatry issued a statement cautioning against the use of tricyclic antidepressants without first weighing the serious and potentially lethal side effects.

In spite of these concerns, the newer antidepressants, called selective serotonin reuptake inhibitors (SSRIs), have become popular and can be a literal lifesaver for some children and their parents. To date, no life-threatening side effects have been associated with the use of SSRIs.

It is a parent's obligation to actively partner with physicians and mental health professionals and not blindly fear the use of antidepressants or other treatments with children. Parents must be wise and reasonable when considering various treatment interventions. Parents know their child better than any professional. Most professionals welcome such partnering and respect parents who question or even obtain second opinions when the welfare of their child is at stake. If you happen to meet a professional who takes offense or is rude in response to your assertiveness, consider switching professionals. Your child's health comes first.

### SUMMARY

- As many as one in eleven children may experience some form of clinical depression before the age of fourteen.
- The *DSM-IV* lists nine symptoms for clinical depression that apply to both adults and children, but some authors have listed as many as forty-six symptoms.
- There are several types of depressive illnesses. The most commonly diagnosed are unipolar depression, bipolar depression, dysthymia, depression NOS, and adjustment disorder with depressed mood.
- Clinical depression is sometimes confused with normal sadness.
- There are four areas where symptoms of depression manifest themselves in children: physically, emotionally, cognitively, and behaviorally.

# CHAPTER 3

## THE GOOD NEWS ABOUT
## DEPRESSION PREVENTION

No army can withstand the strength of an idea whose time
has come.

——VICTOR HUGO

### PREVENTION

*Prevention* means reducing the risk for illness or accident.
Regarding depression, if your child has even two of the risk
factors listed in chapter 1, he or she is at risk for the disease
of depression.

The notion of preventing disease or injury is not new.
Since the dawn of civilization, people have attempted to ward
off calamities through ritual, magic, and various other practices. Many ancient religions practiced preventive rituals,
even though the practitioners would not have considered
them as such. For example, ritual cleansing before meals prevented the spread of disease, avoiding the consumption of
pork prevented deadly trichinosis, and wearing silk under-
shirts into battle reduced infection by creating a "clean
wound" if a soldier was struck by an arrow.

Modern prevention began with the scientific discoveries and modern inventions of the nineteenth and twentieth centuries. Microscopes, blood pressure cuffs, and vaccines that could immunize against disease made the notion of preventing illness realistic. Later, the invention of helmets, seat belts, and air bags decreased the number of injuries when using bicycles, motorcycles, and automobiles.

Today, preventing disease has a multifaceted approach. For example, reducing the risk for heart disease, lung cancer, and type II diabetes includes not only medical intervention but also lifestyle changes, such as diet, exercise, and stress reduction. Fifty years ago, most people thought that smoking was harmless and that America's breakfast staple, fried eggs and bacon, was healthy. Now, millions of dollars are spent on antismoking campaigns, and low-fat diets are nearly always prescribed to patients at risk for heart disease. This multifaceted approach assumes that the patient, and not just medical technology, has the means to reduce the risk of disease or recurrence of disease. It implies an *active partnership* between the person at risk and the medical profession.

## DEPRESSION PREVENTION

Today, preventing depression is about as popular as preventing heart disease fifty years ago. Most people don't think about preventing depression unless the disease strikes a family member. To date, there are no official guidelines for depression prevention, and prevention research is still in its infancy.

In spite of these realities, the field of depression prevention has made progress in recent years and has yielded some good news for the average parent.

The literature on depression prevention encompasses

three types of prevention: primary, secondary, and tertiary. Primary prevention aims at reducing the likelihood of depression in those who have not yet experienced the illness. Secondary prevention aims at increasing the ability to detect the illness early so that it can be properly treated. Tertiary prevention, also called relapse prevention, aims at reducing the recurrence of the illness once it has been experienced.

Existing medical prevention programs incorporate some or all of these types of prevention. Breast cancer prevention programs include commercials that increase public awareness that the disease exists and can be detected early, ensuring more successful treatment (secondary prevention). Heart disease and lung cancer prevention include public service advertising to "stop smoking" and "don't start smoking" (primary prevention). Relapse prevention programs for substance abuse are examples of tertiary prevention. Often, preventing the onset of a disease and preventing a recurrence require the same behavior changes on the part of the patient. Prevention is a lifelong program of change.

Large-scale depression prevention programs are currently limited to secondary prevention in the form of depression awareness days. In addition, some progressive managed care companies have introduced the practice of screening children of depressed parents for depression in an attempt to intervene early in the disease process.

The notion of relapse prevention is just beginning to be practiced beyond the narrow medication-monitoring model. Cognitive-behavioral treatment is becoming more accepted as a valid form of treatment for depression and can include booster sessions spaced several weeks or months apart for up to a year after recovery.

Primary depression prevention is practically nonexistent, but it is being researched across the globe. Although there is not yet conclusive scientific "proof," the results of these preliminary attempts to prevent the onset of depression in children are very promising.

## PRIMARY DEPRESSION PREVENTION RESEARCH

Three well-known research studies in the area of preventing the onset of depression in children have been published. The first measured the effectiveness of a school-based program. The second measured the effectiveness of a clinic-based family program. The third measured the effectiveness of a parent-coaching program. All three studies had relatively small sample sizes but have since been repeated with different samples, sometimes by different researchers, adding to their credibility.

Martin E. P. Seligman, Ph.D., headed the school-based research study at the University of Pennsylvania. He and his students trained at-risk fifth and sixth graders in cognitive and social problem-solving skills that could be used to change their pessimistic thoughts and deal with family conflict in a constructive manner. These youths were compared to a group of fifth and sixth graders who did not receive training. Those who participated in the training groups experienced fewer depressive symptoms immediately following the program and at the six-month follow-up. A follow-up study two years later indicated that the effects of the prevention program increased with the passage of time.[1] The methods and results of this study were published and later described for laypeople in *The Optimistic Child*.

Since that time, there have been studies on native Chinese children and on low-income minority children in the United

States. The results from these studies generally support Dr. Seligman's findings.[2]

William R. Beardslee, M.D., evaluated the clinic-based family program. The program targeted children of depressed parents. This program used education, relief of feelings of guilt for the parents' illness, and reduction of fears as the tools to prevent depression in the children. Dr. Beardslee's results indicated that children who had been through the program had better adaptive function and better parent-child communication than children who had not been through the program. For the parents in the program, changes in depression-related behaviors and attitudes were positively influencing the outcome for their children.[3] Dr. Beardslee published his work in his book *Out of the Darkened Room*.

Tiffany Field, Ph.D., studied the effectiveness of early intervention with depressed mothers and their infants. Based on her previous research on infant behaviors related to maternal depression, she devised a program where infants were massaged and depressed mothers were directly coached on appropriate parenting behaviors while interacting with their babies. The results were a decrease in infant depressive symptoms and positive biochemical changes. These results and the results of studies that followed suggest that infants and toddlers can be protected from early depressive symptoms *even if* the parent remains depressed or is recovering from the illness. This finding creates great hope for mothers suffering from postpartum depression. It also establishes a mandate to intervene early in the life of both parent and child.[4]

These three research studies formed the basis for several subsequent studies that are, together, slowly accumulating evidence suggesting the need for and the likely ability to prevent the onset of some depressions in children at risk. Take note, *all* these preventive interventions were nonmedical. Most theorists and researchers are now in agreement that such preventive interventions will need to encompass medical, psychological, and social arenas and include community, school, and family-based prevention programs.

### ONGOING HOME PREVENTION

The family is the cornerstone of our society. More than any other force it shapes the attitude, the hopes, the ambitions, and the values of the child.

—LYNDON BAINES JOHNSON

Researchers have also come to an agreement that depression prevention needs to be addressed throughout childhood and not just at certain developmental stages.[5] The idea that children can be taught protective skills throughout life is verified throughout the developmental research literature. At different ages, children learn different things. But more important, *they learn the same things in more complex ways.* Laughing and good humor is learned in infancy and toddlerhood, but if adult depression or family tragedy limits the child's exposure to good humor, that child can still learn various nuances of humor at ages two, three, and four. Clearly, a laughing infant or a temperamentally happy infant has a head start in good humor, but a three-year-old can learn fast. Children continually grow, adapt, and change throughout childhood. This gives preventionists great cause for optimism.

No one is better suited to provide ongoing protective skills for a child than that child's parents. Home is the best place to apply and practice the many skills, interventions, and resilience-promoting parenting techniques known to be helpful in reducing the likelihood of depression in children.

The rest of this book describes four areas where parents can intervene in order to do their part to help prevent the onset or relapse of depressive symptoms in their children. The symbolism of *mind, body, heart,* and *soul* is used in order to reflect how comprehensive and ongoing home prevention needs to become.

This broad scope need not be intimidating or overwhelming. Small changes followed by more changes over the course of your son's or daughter's childhood usually complete the task.

## SUMMARY

- Prevention has been in existence since the dawn of civilization.
- A multifaceted approach is used in disease prevention. The patient partners with the medical profession.
- The notion of depression prevention has evolved only in recent years.
- There are three types of prevention: primary (preventing onset), secondary (early identification), and tertiary (relapse prevention).
- There are three key areas of prevention research: school-based prevention, clinic-based prevention, and parent-coaching interventions.
- Preventive interventions should encompass medical, psychological, and social arenas and include community-, school-, and family-based programs.
- Preventing the onset or recurrence of depression is a process that needs to occur throughout childhood. Parents are best equipped to intervene with their children.

# PART 2

## CREATING HOPE FOR CHILDREN

# CHAPTER 4

---

## HOW TO TEACH PROTECTIVE SKILLS

Do not limit your children to your own learning, for they have
been born in another age.

—ANTHONY DE MELLO, *AWAKENING*

September 14, 2001

Andrew, nine, repeatedly crashed his toy plane into
his Twin Towers souvenir. "Mom, what if we were at
Sbarro's [in the World Trade Center] when the plane hit?"

I felt a lump in my throat and a chill darted down my
spine.

Although we live in the Pacific Northwest, almost
our entire extended family lives in the New York and
Washington, D.C., areas. Andrew's uncle had been one
block away from the towers when the first plane hit. Two
of his aunts and another uncle were involved in the after-
math as trained nurses and a firefighter.

Andrew and his brother, Peter, had been to the World
Trade Center twice during family visits. Eating lunch at
the very top was one of the most memorable experiences of their young lives.

Suddenly, the world they knew was gone.

How can we emotionally prepare children to live with hope and optimism when life can often be unpredictable? How can we influence children so that adversity brings about an inner strength rather than a sense of helpless defeat? How do children learn, and in what ways can we teach them, so that the proper skills are deeply ingrained into the very fabric of their being?

## ADVERSITY

No one would argue that bad things happen to good people. From the simple disappointment of breaking a treasured toy to the catastrophic loss of a loved one, adversity is a part of life. Adversity is also frequently depression's trigger. For most children and adolescents, a depressive episode usually follows a major disappointment. Such children have often experienced a family breakup, family relocation, rejection by peers, and even being bullied in school. Indeed, failures to make the baseball team, breakup of a romantic relationship, and relocation of a best friend have all been implicated as triggers for adolescent suicide.

It is important to remember, then, that reducing the risk for depression begins with preparing children to deal with adversity.

What a child considers adversity is often not what an adult considers adversity. To a toddler, walking is an adversity. If you doubt that, take note how many months and tantrums it takes from the first step to a carefree run across the room. Likewise, to some preschoolers, tying shoes is a major adversity. Homework is an adversity to most school-aged children. Dealing with rejection is a common adversity suffered by young teenagers.

Little adversities help prepare children to deal with bigger ones *if parents allow for and honor the adversity*. Barbara Coloroso, in her book *Parenting through Crisis*, describes how

---

**Something to Think About #2**
*Your Beliefs about Adversity*

What do you consider adversity? Do you believe some people can bounce back from adversity better than others? Do you think there are some things that a person can *never* recover from, such as the death of a loved one, recurrent illness, or depression?

Do you believe adversity is bad, harmful, evil, or just unpleasant?

Are there times when you think other people's difficulties are so minor that they shouldn't complain about them as adversities? Think now about your children's complaints about homework, scheduling, and so on.

---

little difficulties prepared her family to deal with the cataclysmic adversity of one of her children's battle with cancer. She writes that getting through the common childhood afflictions of illness, injuries, and everyday hassles "with optimism and resolve" served as a model for her family when faced with the life-threatening illness.[1]

*Allowing for adversity* means you don't clear the path for a bump-free toddle across the room. You don't tie your child's shoe because it's faster than waiting for him to do it. And you don't do your child's homework. Instead, *let the child do it.* That way the experience of overcoming adversity is attained. Please take note that you might sometimes need to encourage and help just enough so that the adversity is overcome. But even if you do help, be sure to give your child the credit: "You did it. Good job!"

*Honoring adversity* means stepping out of your own beliefs about what constitutes adversity and empathizing with the child's beliefs. For example:

Laurie, nine: "Nancy won't play with me! I'm all alone. Why did this have to happen? Now I have nothing to do! This is the worst day of my life!"

Mom: "Nancy won't play with you? How terrible! Tell me about it."

Eventually, Mom will need to guide Laurie toward overcoming the adversity she presents (with skills learned later in this book). But for now, listening to *Laurie's perspective* is more important. It conveys to Laurie that her experience is valid and that Mom is willing to honor it.

---

### Something You Can Do #5
#### *Listen to Your Child's Perspective*

Spend a little extra time listening for your child's perspective on events. Show that you understand his perspective by validating feelings and clarifying words ("So you're saying that . . .") or by repeating what he has said (like Mom did with Laurie in the example).

If the situation is an adversity for your child and you can't or won't make the situation easier (such as not doing your child's homework), *still* validate her viewpoint. Then, let her know you believe she is strong enough to overcome the situation. Support her, if necessary, but don't rescue her.

Later, when she has succeeded (in spite of complaints, moans, and groans), remind her of her success without commenting on any unpleasantness in the process. For example, "Boy, that was hard for you. But I knew you could do it."

---

Repeated experiences of conquering adversities create what Martin E. P. Seligman, Ph.D., calls "mastery experiences." Over time, these mastery experiences can create an inner resilience that enables a child to bounce back from the more difficult adversities of adolescence and adulthood. Resilience is one of the hallmarks of a depression-free child.

## MASTER OF UNCONSCIOUS EXPERIENCE

As a young therapist, I was introduced to the ideas and therapeutic techniques of Milton H. Erickson, M.D. Dr. Erickson was an innovative hypnotist and psychiatrist who taught and practiced from the mid-1930s until his death in 1980. He was known as the "master of the unconscious." So great was his reputation that other psychiatrists would sometimes travel great distances with their most difficult patients in order for those patients to be seen by him for treatment.

Abandoning the lofty theories of current psychiatric thought, Dr. Erickson practiced his psychotherapeutic art from the commonsense principles of human nature. Having spent much of his early life recovering from a severe bout of paralyzing polio, he knew firsthand about the nature of adversity and the learning process. Indeed, he retaught himself to *walk*, step by step. For years, Dr. Erickson would remark that his personal, direct experience with polio was his most important teacher.

Based on his experience, Dr. Erickson also believed that an unconscious mind exists, which learns in different and more powerful ways than the conscious mind. Today's advances in neuroscience are validating many of his hypotheses about learning and the unconscious.

## THE NATURE OF LEARNING

Children have never been very good at listening to their elders, but they have never failed to imitate them.

—JAMES BALDWIN

Contrary to some schools of thought, the unconscious is not a mysterious place deep within the recesses of the mind that only the carefully trained dare go exploring. *Unconscious* simply means as it reads. It is learning that occurs *without one's awareness.*

There is a simple neurological explanation for the existence of the unconscious. Information is processed at different speeds and intensities in different parts of the brain. Often, by the time the "thinking brain"(where we experience consciousness) is turned on, the "emotional brain" has already processed the information. So your heart will pound *before* you realize the man in the shadows is simply your neighbor. For a few seconds, you act unconsciously. Likewise, if you are deeply engrossed in reading this book, you might not be consciously aware of a clock ticking, furnace running, or cars whizzing by on a nearby street until I direct your attention to them. But I assure you, the information is being processed out of your momentary awareness. Neuroscience is just beginning to scratch the surface of understanding the brain's complexity.

An example of unconscious learning is the return of a childhood geographic accent. I have a distinctly New York accent. But since I have now lived in the Pacific Northwest for more years than I lived out East, most of the time it is barely noticeable because I have unconsciously adapted the local accent. During the months following the September 11 terrorist attacks, my childhood accent "slipped out," and I began to receive comments about it from clients and acquaintances. Soon I realized that, *although I wasn't aware of it,* I was identifying with my family and history as a New Yorker even though that family and the events were miles away.

Often our deepest beliefs, attitudes, habits, and even thoughts are the product of unconscious, often emotional, learning. *With regard to depression, parents often unconsciously pass on depression-promoting habits and thoughts to their children who then learn those same habits and thoughts unconsciously.* In the next chapter, I will examine this process and offer some suggestions to counter it.

Conscious learning is learning that occurs *with awareness.* Reading this book is a form of conscious learning. You read the words, think about them, and then think about how they may apply to your situation. When you do the exercises in this book—a way for me to provide you with direct experience—you *consciously choose* to do the exercises. They don't just happen. Eventually, as you practice these skills over and over in the emotional heat of daily life, you may find that you occasionally practice them without awareness. At that point, your conscious learning has become unconscious, or automatic. Congratulations! You've formed a good habit.

These two types of learning are important to remember when considering how best to teach protective skills to your children. Each form of learning is important but *emotional unconscious learning is experienced more deeply over time.* From most to least powerful, the ways children learn are by

- direct experience (unconscious)
- modeling (unconscious)
- education (conscious)

Below are examples of each of these types of learning.

## Direct Experience

"JASON HOT," Mom says as her three-year-old approaches the turned-on stove. "NO, NO—HOT."

As Mom reaches out to stop him, Jason playfully lunges forward, putting his hand on the stove. A piercing scream follows.

Cold water and hugs nurse the minor burn.

Fifteen minutes later, Jason points to the stove and says, "HOT—BURN—NO—NO."

Jason has just learned from direct experience (unconsciously and then consciously) something his mom was attempting to teach him (consciously). An accidental minor burn conveyed the message much more powerfully. More important, Jason also learned, via direct experience, that pain can be comforted. Mom nurtured, cared for, and comforted him when he was burned. While I do *not* advocate purposely burning your child in order to teach him not to touch the stove, I offer the example to demonstrate this type of learning.

## Modeling

For several weeks I had been trying to get my son Andrew, age four, to stop biting his nails. Scolding, rewards, and drawing his attention to the behavior didn't help. The fancy behavior-modification techniques also didn't work. Then as therapist-moms often do, I analyzed his behavior: Was he anxious? What was causing the stress? Did something bad happen to him? Was I too strict a parent?

One day, while stuck in traffic, I glanced over and noticed his fingers in his mouth. I was about to point this out to him when I noticed I also had my fingers in my mouth!

Within one month, both Andrew and I had beautiful nails. The best part was Andrew never knew that his behavior had been changed through my intervention. I simply kept my fingers away from my mouth and he naturally stopped without effort or thought.

Andrew's learning was unconscious and as such was effortless for him. We often underestimate this powerful form of learning. In this book, I will emphasize it. By the way, it has now been several years since these events took place. Andrew and I still have great nails.

## Education

The teacher smiles, looks at her pupils, and says in a pleasant voice, "What is two plus two?"

"Four," reply the students.

"What is four plus five?"

A brief pause is followed by, "Nine."

Education is the primary method of learning used in schools, universities, and even prevention programs across the United States. Unlike unconscious learning, it requires effort to learn in this way. One must think, reason, and then apply the concepts to everyday life.

Conscious learning is vitally important. It is the type of learning that puts us above the rest of the animal kingdom. But it is also the *least* powerful method of learning. That is why most things learned consciously must be practiced. A child must practice reading in order to read. An adult must practice exercising in order to develop a healthy routine. A person must practice nondepressive ways of thinking in order to feel good.

The role of formal education is to provide form and structure to a more comprehensive learning process that actually occurs consciously and unconsciously. A child in the classroom may be consciously focusing on mathematical equations, but she is simultaneously learning, without conscious focus, how to give directions with a smile, good eye contact, and a pleasant voice and how to behave in a group setting. The experience and atmosphere of the classroom is just as much a teaching tool as the actual lesson plan.

As a parent in the role of teaching your children depression-resisting skills, you need to keep in mind this process of *multilevel learning*. Doing so will make your teaching more effective.

### THE THREE TEACHING PRINCIPLES

In his book *Experiencing Erickson*, Jeffrey Zeig, Ph.D., outlines three principles that Dr. Milton Erickson kept in mind while treating his patients. First, change is gradual. Second, experiences must be created or used to facilitate the best learning. And third, a person's strengths (yes, plural) must be the foundation of a person's experience of learning.[2]

1. Change is gradual.
2. Create and use experiences.
3. Build on strengths.

### Change Is Gradual

Learning and change are gradual processes that occur over and over at many developmental stages in a child's life. Indeed, many times the things learned at one age need to be

---

**Something You Can Do #6**
*Teach without Speaking*

Notice your child's mannerisms, facial expressions, language phrases, tones of voice, and so on. Which adult in the home has those same ways of expressing himself or herself? Also notice use or lack of use of manners, considerate behavior, and so on. Which adult in the home models those same behaviors?

Identify one habit or mannerism you would like to change in your child.

For two months, *consistently* act in the way you would like your child to act. For example, say "please" and "thank you" or speak softly if this is the behavior you would like to see in your children. If you slip up, gently correct yourself in front of your child.

You don't need to tell him about your efforts or correct him any differently about his poor behaviors. Simply notice whether your child changes without being "taught."

---

unlearned and replaced by new discoveries at a different age. At one year old, a child eats with his hands, but at three years old, with a fork. At five years old, a child reads with a parent, but at seven, he reads alone. At six most children view kissing and hugging at face value in all situations. By twelve, all but a very few understand that some of these affectionate expressions are sexual in nature.

Children as well as adults learn, unlearn, and relearn continuously. This is good news if you or your child currently has depression-promoting habits or thoughts. Mistakes in learning that lead to depression can be unlearned and replaced by healthier, more positive learning. So, even if your child has already experienced depression, there is reason to believe a second episode can be avoided or certainly lessened in intensity by effectively teaching your child protective skills (consciously and unconsciously).

This notion of gradual change is also consoling because there is no need to feel that a setback is a failure. Relapses to unhelpful patterns of thought and behavior are reflections of the learning process. *In this model of prevention, mistakes are accepted and used for the purpose of relearning skills in a more profound manner.*

## Create and Use Experiences
When teaching your children any of the skills in chapters 6 through 9, keep in mind that they will learn better if they discover the skill for themselves. For example:

> "Jeremy keeps getting me in trouble," says Allison, age seven.
>
> "What does he do?" asks Dad.
>
> "He pokes at me in class. I yell. The teacher sees me and I get in trouble."
>
> "Have you told the teacher?"
>
> "Yes. She doesn't believe me. She says I can't yell in class."

In this case, if Allison's father marches into the school, talks to the teacher, and sets things straight, Allison will learn (unconsciously) that grown-ups (specifically dads) will rescue her from her problems. In other words, she is helpless to solve her own problems. In some cases, parents need to rescue their children—but not in this case. Rescuing should only occur if the situation threatens the child's integrity or well-being.

If Allison's father tells Allison to poke Jeremy back,

Allison still has not solved her own problem. Instead, she learns (unconsciously) to depend on someone bigger and stronger to tell her what to do.

If Allison's father tells Allison to solve her own problem or to quit being a crybaby, Allison—who doesn't yet have the social skill of assertiveness—will still learn helplessness, a hallmark and risk factor of depression.

*Creating an experience* that allows Allison to learn the skill *on her own* is a powerful way of teaching. In this case, initiating a game of poking at the dinner table can affect such experiential learning. If Allison's father suddenly began to gently and playfully poke Allison at the dinner table, he would elicit her natural response. She would yell just as she does in school. From there, alternatives can be explored and taught.

"Is that what happens in school?" asks Dad.

"Yes. *That's* how I get into trouble!"

"But yelling doesn't work. What else can you do?" Allison's father gently and playfully pokes her repeatedly.

Allison, who now joins in the game, giggles out loud.

Allison's father stops poking. "Will giggling work?"

"No."

Allison's father begins poking again and Allison, now frustrated, hits him.

"What will happen if you hit Jeremy in class?" he asks.

"I'll get in trouble again," says Allison, now red with anger.

Allison's father begins the playful poke again and says, "Now think, Allison. What can you do that won't get you in trouble?"

After exhausting a few more poor responses, Allison raises her hand high and straight over her head and leaves it in that position.

Surprised, Allison's father asks, "What are you doing?"

Allison replies, "Telling the teacher that Jeremy is poking me and I don't want to get in trouble again!"

Allison's father replies, "Now, that might work. Want to try it?"

"Okay."

Notice that Allison's father left the solution as something Allison might try. This leaves room for the possibility that she might need to rework a different solution later.

Creating experiences can take five or ten extra minutes of your dinnertime, but its effect is profound. In this case, Allison thought of a plan: raise her hand in class and tell the teacher what is happening when it is happening. She thought of that plan out of her *personal experience,* during a role-play exercise. In that, she learned an assertiveness skill both consciously and unconsciously. Allison also learned unconsciously that she need not be a victim by suffering needlessly in class or depending on someone bigger and stronger to rescue her. She experienced her problem in a safe setting, struggled through the adversity (getting poked), and came up with a solution. If her solution fails in the classroom, her father left the door open for further discussion or action. This sends Allison another unconscious message that her feelings count and her eventual overcoming of this adversity means something to her father.

## Build on Strengths

In an era when medical and mental health professionals were trained only in identifying and treating pathology—most are still trained that way—Dr. Erickson believed that every person had inherent strengths that could be used to create a good outcome. He once "cured" a woman with severe depression by noticing that even as she remained locked in her house with curtains drawn, she tenderly cared for a lovely African violet on her windowsill. He recognized that this very severely depressed woman had a nurturing quality. Instead of interpreting this quality as a weakness that aided her depression, he considered it her strength. His intervention consisted of expanding on this strength. Dr. Erickson simply convinced her that she should put her ability to good service. He instructed her to grow more African violets and donate a plant to each person experiencing a major event at her church. Soon, she was providing flowers for baptisms, weddings, and funerals. This, eventually, required that she leave her house and interact with other people. When the woman finally died of old age years later, she earned a full-page write-up in the local newspaper, with the heading "The African Violet Queen of Milwaukee."[3]

All children have strengths and weaknesses, good sides and bad sides. Even the weaknesses can become strengths if properly utilized. We all know the story of Rudolph the red-nosed reindeer. And, in Walt Disney's movie *Dumbo,* the elephant's large ears, which were such a glaring weakness by traditional standards, became Dumbo's greatest strength with the help of one visionary little mouse.

Parents can be visionary in evaluating their children's so-called negative traits. Needy and dependent children can become people oriented. Oppositional or strong-willed children can become feisty with leadership qualities. Shy children can become careful. Depressive and pessimistic children can become tempered realists. Weaknesses can become strengths. Later I will describe in more detail how parents' interpretation of their children's behavior can shape those children's outlook about themselves and life. *Patterned* parental interpretations can either help or hinder a child's ability to resist depression.

---

### Something You Can Do #7
*Reinterpret Weaknesses as Strengths*

Make a list of your child's irritating, negative, or difficult patterns of behavior. After each, list three ways that negative pattern can be reinterpreted as something positive. Be behaviorally specific. ("You're a great kid" is *not* a reinterpretation of behavior.) For example:

Negative pattern: "Jessica complains."

Reinterpretation: "Jessica is assertive." "Jessica doesn't keep her feelings inside where they might fester." "By complaining, Jessica opens the door to communicate with me. She has the potential to become a good communicator."

---

## UTILIZING ADVERSITY

People in this country do not generally handle adversity well. We panic, become anxious or depressed, or complain and whine about how "this shouldn't happen." We think of adversity as bad and something to be avoided at all cost. We have been aptly called "the feel-good people" in a "rich country."

Attempting to avoid adversity is about as useless as trying to stop breathing. Go ahead, try to stop breathing. It is better to accept adversity as a given and develop healthier ways to live within that reality. Knowing which adversities are avoidable, which are not, and which we create ourselves by our own poor choices are skills that develop over time.

Many people accustomed to adversity have learned to live well and do not become chronically anxious or depressed. Dr. Erickson, whom I mentioned earlier, not only suffered repeated hospitalizations and chronic pain from post-polio syndrome but also lived with half a diaphragm, spinal arthritis, emphysema, severe allergies, and lifelong problems with partial paralysis. In addition, he was color blind, was tone deaf, had double vision, and once suffered diphtheria. Yet, in training videos recorded in his seventies, he seems almost radiant with boyish playfulness as he works with people from his wheelchair. Dr. Erickson surely had his moments of discouragement, anger, frustration, and grief, but over the years—gradually—he learned to use even severe adversity to his own and to others' benefit.

Another example is actor Christopher Reeve, who played Superman in the 1970s and 1980s. Paralyzed from the neck down in an accident, he wrote two books and has championed the cause of spinal-cord injury recovery and research. During the writing of this book, he created a stir in the medical profession by experiencing sensations and slight movement where before none existed. Adversity may have changed how he conducts his life, but it certainly hasn't defeated him. Instead, he uses adversity to inspire others with similar adversities.

There are countless examples of people, famous and not famous, who have dealt with chronic or serious adversity and remained happy, productive, and giving. Teaching your children about their lives and holding them up as role models can inspire your children to overcome their own adversities.

Children who grow up believing that adversities are problems to be solved, difficulties to be overcome, or experiences to be lived through and gained from are less likely to experience some forms of depression than children who believe adversities are insurmountable.

In the opening example, my son Andrew was traumatized by the events of September 11, 2001. Using many of the principles outlined here, I assisted him in resolving his feelings about the events. I honored his perspective, allowed him

---

### Something You Can Do #8
#### *Create Role Models*

Identify your child's adversities. Does he have a chronic medical illness or mental health diagnosis? Does she have a history of abuse or trauma? Has he suffered a recent disappointment? Has she been the victim of discrimination or cruel words?

Find examples of people who have experienced similar adversities and overcome them. Read about them to your child. Use the Internet or library to obtain information about each person. Some examples of people who have overcome adversity are Bill Russell, Jesse Owens, Dennis Chavez, and Rosa Parks (discrimination); Eleanor Roosevelt and Apollo Anton Ohno (difficult childhoods); Helen Keller and Christopher Reeve (physical disabilities); Winston Churchill (stuttering and depression); and Marie Osmond and Franklin D. Roosevelt (depression).

Perhaps in your own family, there is an aunt, uncle, grandparent, or ancestor who overcame hardship and could serve as a more personal role model. Immigrant parents or grandparents who overcame obstacles and bettered their lives are examples. Tell their stories with a triumphant twist!

---

to express his feelings, and modeled realistic optimism even in the midst of my own tears. Within two weeks, Andrew stopped crashing his planes into his souvenir. He also stopped drawing picture after picture of the Twin Towers. Instead he decided, "They can't stop us. We will build something even bigger and better."

Developmentally, the experience ushered Andrew into a new awareness that the world is not confined to his school, friends, and sports events. He began to watch the world news on television every two or three days (monitored by a parent) and read the Sunday paper to keep up with current events. Eventually, this led to many discussions about making the world a better place and about realistic ways he might contribute to its betterment.

For Andrew, this was a relatively minor adversity. All of our extended family survived and remained safe through the crisis. But what is important is that he worked through the adversity *himself* (with a little encouragement) and actually grew from the experience. It is the best a parent can hope for their children: adversity used to effect a positive result.

## SUMMARY

- Children learn (from most to least powerful) through direct experience (unconscious), modeling (unconscious), and education (conscious).
- The three principles to remember when teaching skills to your children: (1) change is gradual, (2) create and use experiences, and (3) build on strengths.
- Personal weaknesses can be used as strengths.
- Adversity happens and can be used to foster a depression-resistant inner strength in your child.
- Allow minor adversities to be experienced by your children. If necessary, coach them to persevere through the experience.
- Once an adversity has been lived through or conquered, discuss with your child ways in which he or she has grown from the experience.

# CHAPTER 5

## BUT WAIT! WHAT IF THE *PARENT* IS DEPRESSED?

In the depths of winter I finally learned there was in me an invincible summer.

—ALBERT CAMUS

Aside from experiencing an episode of depression, the most serious risk factor for a child is having a depressed parent. In fact, some studies indicate that a child of a depressed parent has a *41 to 77 percent chance* of experiencing depression or some other psychiatric or behavioral disturbance.[1] This statistic is not due to genetics alone. The *Harvard Mental Health Letter* puts pure heritability at 50 percent for unipolar depression.[2] It is higher for bipolar depression. The other 50 percent is due to environmental influences as discussed in chapter 1. Parents pass on to their children ways of thinking and behaving that encourage and sustain depression. In this chapter, we will explore how a parent's depression or parenting style can influence the development of depression in their children and what can be done about it.

## DESTRUCTIVE PATTERNS

- "I can't take it anymore."
- "Why does it have to be this way?"
- "I must be the worst parent in the world."
- "I should have never had kids."
- "What's wrong with me?"
- "What's wrong with my child?"
- "Why did I get stuck with *this* child?"
- "I hate my life."
- "They'd be better off without me."
- "This is too hard."

These are some of an endless number of self-defeating thoughts that can play over and over again in a depressed parent's mind. And the depression need not be a serious, lay-in-the-bed-all-day clinical depression. Even mildly depressed parents, parents recovering from a depressive episode, or parents who have nonclinical depressive symptoms can pass down unhelpful ways of thinking and behaving. When a parent's attitude is self-defeating, the child may take on the same style through modeling and the direct experience of being parented with pessimism (unconscious learning). In addition, if a parent is consistently self-absorbed, preoccupied, or withdrawn, the child may not receive adequate attention and affection. Children are, by their very nature, time consuming and needy.

This is not to assume that only depressed parents yield depressed children. Sometimes children become depressed without a parent's influence. Genetics, temperament, social climate, or uniquely personal struggles can trigger depression in a child even when the parents are happy, optimistic, and nurturing. An example of this will be described in chapter 9.

However, the evidence is very clear that depression runs in families. Parents can contribute to the development of depression in their children by their attitudes, beliefs, and behavior.

Very young children recognize depression in their parents and can demonstrate depressive symptoms in response. Researchers M. Katherine Weinberg, Ph.D., and Edward Z. Tronick, Ph.D., have observed infants as young as three months old who are able to detect depression in their mothers. In their study, infants of depressed mothers looked at their mothers less frequently, engaged with objects less frequently, and showed more negative and irritable behaviors. Even the infants' biology changed. They had higher heart rates and cortisol levels. Cortisol is a chemical related to stress and also depression.[3]

These changes are not necessarily permanent, however. As reviewed in chapter 3, Tiffany Field, Ph.D., has observed improvements in infants whose parents learn and practice proper interacting skills, even if they remain somewhat depressed.[4] It is not necessarily the diagnosis of depression in a parent that determines the outcome for the child. Rather, it is the *parent's behavior even if depressed*. Evidence suggests that a parent who musters the energy to positively engage with his or her child may actually provide the child with some protective learning that could help prevent the spread of depression in the family.

Several years ago, I learned firsthand about passing on depression-promoting ways of thinking and behaving to my children. An epiphany occurred one morning when I found a raw egg, minus the shell, on the kitchen floor. A bowl and an eggshell were on the messy kitchen countertop. The usually ever-present and talkative Andrew, then four, was not to be found. His brother, Peter, then one, was napping.

"Andrew, where are you?" I called.

No answer.

I looked around the nearby rooms and found Andrew curled up in the large rocking chair in the family room. He had tears in his eyes.

"Andrew, there's an egg on the floor."

He threw his arms around me and sobbed in frustration, "I can't do it. I just can't." He was referring to cracking and scrambling eggs.

The thought "I can't do it" had been a constant companion in my mind for years. It popped into my mind whenever a difficulty or challenge presented itself. The knee-jerk response usually resulted in a decision to give up and let someone else take care of the difficulty or meet the challenge. Here now was my oldest son stating the very same words and giving up his challenge as he developed his own self-defeating belief.

Parents do influence the development of depression-promoting or depression-resisting thought patterns and behaviors in their children. And if infants as young as three months old are being affected, we can assume that children are not learning these patterns through conscious reasoning. Rather, they are learning unconsciously through modeling and direct experience.

This need not be discouraging. All that is needed is *awareness* that self-defeating thoughts, actions, and phrases are going to slip out whether you yourself have been parented in depression-promoting ways or whether you have experienced episodes of depression and/or anxiety. The important thing lies in being sure to *self-correct* when you make such a mistake.

Suffice it to say, Andrew cracked several eggs that morning, which were saved for later baking. In fact, cracking and scrambling eggs became his special job for several weeks, providing plenty of experience. Back pats, attaboys, and comments about how, with practice, he would get the hang of it were sprinkled generously through the process. Weeks and months later, I occasionally reminded Andrew of the time he thought he couldn't crack and scramble eggs. He smiled triumphantly.

---

### Something You Can Do #9
*The Success Journal*

In a spiral notebook, record examples of your child's personal struggles that resulted in your child learning a new skill. Learning to scramble eggs is an example. So is learning to ride a bike, read, do math, fly a kite, and color inside the lines. Older children learn how to do well on tests, play sports, dance, play a musical instrument, prevent a fistfight with peers, and make new friends.

Make sure you record ordinary life experiences that required practice or repeated attempts. Make note of any self-doubt your child had *before* succeeding. Then make note of how he or she felt *after* success was achieved.

Keep the journal for times when your child is discouraged about a new challenge. At those times, sit with your child and use the journal to reminisce.

---

### GUILTY PARENTS

Our greatest glory is not in never falling, but in rising every time we fall.

—CONFUCIUS

Now, lest you think my epiphany of my passing on depression-promoting patterns to my children cured me of my bad habit, I confess it hasn't. For example, the thought "I can't do it" is still a constant knee-jerk companion that pops up when things get tough. The difference now is that when I slip up, especially if I speak the words in front of my children, *I notice* or my husband or children notice and speak up! Then, I self-correct, sometimes with a little help ("Mom, never say *never!*").

Being aware of how we, as parents, contribute to our children's vulnerability for depression can cause some guilt. Depressed parents tend to exact severe judgment on themselves when they act in unwanted ways ("I'm dysfunctional, sick, bad, terrible . . ."). This, in turn, can increase the unwanted parent-child interactions.

A colleague, Bernie Busch, L.I.C.S.W., once told me his rule of thumb for practicing parenting skills. He would tell his clients that if they practiced good parenting skills *60 percent of the time,* chances were their children would turn out okay. He called this "the 60 percent rule" and encouraged many a discouraged parent with the notion. I pass his wisdom on to you.

Remember, mistakes and setbacks are considered normal opportunities in a world where change is gradual and *no one* is perfect. Success for you, as a parent, occurs *each time* you catch a depression-promoting attitude, comment, or action, and turn it around such as I did in the scrambled-eggs incident. Over the years, my children have watched me self-correct so many times it has become almost a game. In turn, I playfully help them self-correct in the hope that, over the years, the skill will become automatic for them. (See "Something You Can Do #10.)

## PATTERNED JUDGMENTS

Before specifically examining how parental interpretations of children's behavior shape children's beliefs, take the time to consider "Something to Think About #3."

## Something You Can Do #10
### *Become Aware*

Over the next two weeks, write down your knee-jerk responses—thoughts and behaviors—to events that occur in your life. Are they self-defeating or self-empowering?

After those two weeks, observe and write down your child's knee-jerk responses to events in his or her life. Again, note if they are self-defeating or self-empowering.

This will prepare you for exercises described in chapter 7 and cue you to areas where you can help your child come up with empowering responses where self-defeating ones usually occur.

## Something to Think About #3
### *Insecurity's Bad Influence*

*All* parents feel insecure about their ability to parent. There can be an added insecurity if your own parenting was less than optimal. Some parents allow their insecurities to influence their interactions with their own children. They *avoid their children* or conversely *become overinvolved* out of fear their child might become like them. Research has actually identified these two opposite parenting styles as common in families affected with depression.[5] The methods of avoiding or becoming overinvolved are endless.

If you tend to avoid or become overinvolved with your children, begin to think about specific ways to change. This chapter and also chapters 8 and 9 will provide you with some ideas.

I once went to a professional workshop about oppositional-defiant children. Oppositional defiant disorder (ODD)
describes a particular set of symptoms and behavior problems found in some children. The speaker at the workshop proceeded to explain that you could always tell an
oppositional-defiant child from a normal child (as if such a
differentiation exists) by the following:

> All the children are lined up at the classroom door for
> lunch and everyone is about ready to walk out the door.
> The oppositional-defiant child is the one who trips and
> spills an entire sixty-four-pack of crayons on the floor,
> causing mass pandemonium and a delayed lunch as
> teachers regain control of the class.

The first tragedy in this presentation was that the speaker
used a mental health diagnosis, a tool that provides a working
hypothesis for treatment, as a subtly derogatory label. This
negative interpretation of a child's behavior was solely based
on *the speaker's* training, beliefs, and life orientation—not the
child's state of being. In reality, the child in the example he
provided could have been tired, distracted, or even anxious.

The second tragedy in this example was that the teachers
and parents listening to this authoritative speaker laughed
heartily, as if the speaker were touching on something they
all knew to be true about this "type" of child. The audience
had adapted the judgmental meaning the presenter suggested. In turn, these teachers and parents could unwittingly
begin to treat children displaying some of these behaviors in
prejudicial and derogatory ways whether or not those children met the criteria for the actual diagnosis of ODD. This is
one of the ways children with mental health diagnoses are
put at risk for depression.

By a similar process, depressed parents can negatively

interpret their children's mistakes and behaviors based on *their* beliefs, childhood experiences of being parented, or life orientation. They, like the speaker, can form prejudicial impressions of their children and treat them accordingly. Subsequently, the children can unwittingly take on the parents' beliefs and impressions and make them their own—and act accordingly. This then becomes the vicious cycle of self-fulfilling prophecy.

Research indicates that, when compared to nondistressed and nondepressed parents, distressed and depressed parents are more likely to interpret their children's mistakes negatively and correct their children in inappropriate ways. Children's behaviors also tend to be worse when living with a distressed or depressed parent.[6]

There are two ways parents can pass on depression-promoting patterns to children. The first, discussed at the beginning of this chapter, is through modeling. The second is through criticizing, labeling, and punishing instead of using teaching methods of correction when children fail. An example of criticizing rather than teaching is as follows:

> Mary, age eight, spills her glass of milk.
> Dad or Mom instantly responds, "What a mess! I told you to be more careful! What's the matter with you?"

By contrast, a teaching response would be:

> "Whoops. Get some paper towels, quick!" followed by showing the child how to clean up the mess.

Mistakes often occur in life and are repeated throughout life. Many adults have spilled full glasses of assorted liquids over the breakfast table.

The following is a list of critical patterns versus educational patterns that are often used when a child makes mistakes.

| Critical Patterns | Educational Patterns |
|---|---|
| Yelling | Seeing your child's perspective |
| Blaming | Problem solving |
| Giving up in disgust when your child's problem is repetitive | Persisting and trying again to teach your child in a different way than the time before |
| Punishing without thinking through how the punishment will teach a lesson | Providing consequences that teach a better behavior while explaining why the new behavior is better (example: We eat without silliness so we don't choke on our food.) |
| Withholding affection from your child | Demonstrating affection or, if you are not the affectionate type, providing pats and words of encouragement |

If your parenting style tends to run down the left-hand column *and* you are also experiencing depressive symptoms (see chapter 2), it is time to consider professional help.

Sometimes depression-promoting patterns are simply a matter of needing to learn new parenting strategies. Critical and punishing parenting styles, after all, are traditional and still advocated in some religious and societal circles. As you read the next four chapters dedicated to teaching your children protective skills, notice how all the examples of parenting are educational in style. In addition, some parenting books that advocate an educational style of parenting are listed in the "Resources" section.

For the purposes of preventing depression in your children, begin to practice this next "Something You Can Do" activity.

---

## Something You Can Do #11
### *Catch Your Critical Thoughts*

Whenever your child makes a mistake, practice saying nothing until you take two deep breaths. During the two deep breaths, again, *pay attention to your own knee-jerk thoughts.* If those instant thoughts are critical, accusing, or otherwise not educational, ask yourself, *What skill does my child need to learn?* After you have calmed yourself and answered that question, call to mind the most pleasant moment that occurred between you and your child within the last two or three days. *Then* address your child with, "It's wrong to [insert mistake—examples: throw food on the floor; talk back to me]." Then, provide task correction: "Take these paper towels and wipe up this mess" or "Repeat your words to me in a more respectful manner."

---

The next section is devoted to seeking professional help for your depression as a means of reducing the risk of depression for your children.

### RESISTANCE TO DEPRESSION TREATMENT

"I'm not depressed," snarled Mr. O'Neill. "The kid is a waste. If he'd shape up, the whole household would be fine."

Mr. O'Neill had brought his preteen son to a therapist's office. The child was failing two classes, spending more and more time in his room, and arguing with his parents. Mr. O'Neill was noticeably irritable, brooding, critical, and very pessimistic. In addition, he had reported losing weight, not sleeping well, and not wanting to socialize like he used to. The therapist had correctly noticed that, in addition to the problems with his son, Mr. O'Neill seemed depressed, and she gently recommended a thorough assessment. Mr. O'Neill, not aware of his own state of being, totally blamed and focused on his son.

Parental depression can be triggered by a number of things, including the chronic stress of living in a difficult situation or with a challenging child. Having a child with a medical or mental health diagnosis automatically puts a parent at risk for depression. This is so widely accepted that several managed care companies automatically send out depression screening questionnaires to parents if their child is diagnosed with certain medical or mental health problems.

Still, resistance to the treatment of parental depression exists, and this resistance is the unwelcome guest in many therapists' offices. There are many reasons for this resistance to treatment. First and foremost, it is human nature to resist change. Most people experience themselves a certain way and tend to stay with what is familiar.

The second major reason parents resist their own treatment is a lack of awareness that how they are experiencing life is not the same as how other people are experiencing life. Often, other people notice someone is depressed based on observations of that person. The person himself, however, may not see it.

Aside from these two reasons, there are an infinite number of personal protests that prevent parents from seeking help for their own depression. The most common protests are really common fears:

- fear of being weak
- fear of being "diseased"

- fear of being judged or labeled
- fear of the treatments themselves
- fear of being diagnosed in some form of medical record
- fear of lifestyle disruptions

Some of these fears are not totally irrational. Some people who are diagnosed with clinical depression *are* judged and labeled, sometimes by the very health care professionals to whom they turn for help. They certainly need to make lifestyle changes. But being "weak" or "diseased" is a matter of perspective, and fear of treatment usually eases when treatment is understood.

The bottom line is that if a person has mild to moderate depressive symptoms and negative thought patterns, early treatment can prevent a more serious depressive episode later. Risking a serious depressive episode once aware of mild depressive symptoms is downright foolish and poor modeling for children.

## OVERCOMING RESISTANCE

Awareness, awareness, awareness.

—ANTHONY DE MELLO, *AWAKENING*

There are two sure ways to overcome resistance. The first, and the most common method, is to wait until the symptoms become so serious that a major crisis occurs, catapulting one into reality and treatment. This method is in line with general societal practice. First the United States is attacked on home soil, *and then* a Department of Homeland Security is created. First heart disease becomes the number-one killer, *and then* prevention programs are launched. First thousands of fifteen- and sixteen-year-olds die in automobile accidents, *and then* the age for driving unsupervised with friends is raised.

Obviously, I am not in favor of this after-the-fact method of overcoming resistance to depression treatment. And if you are reading this after suffering the results of this after-the-fact method—suicide attempt, complete emotional breakdown, loss of children through abuse or neglect, loss of job through poor performance, loss of friends or spouse because of being so negative, down, or critical—you probably agree with me.

By contrast, the preferred method of overcoming resistance is actually much easier than the first: awareness. Begin by paying attention to your thoughts, feelings, and behaviors and how they affect your loved ones. Do your children feel comfortable talking to you when they have difficulties? Or do they avoid you when you are in a bad mood? Has your significant other complained recently about your moods, your irritability or temper, or your inability to hear his or her perspective on situations? Do you find yourself having less patience with your children, less time or interest in playing with them? Do you feel more guilt about how you have been recently parenting, especially if the parenting style is not typical for you? Once you begin to *really notice* the profound and subtle ways you set the emotional tone in your home by your mood, your language, your tone of voice, and your facial expressions, you have begun to overcome your personal resistance to intervention.

The second step is to acknowledge that any and all problems can't be solely the other person's fault. It takes two to tango.

The third step is to realize that you can't manage something as complex as clinical depression by yourself. Seek professional help. Your well-being and *that of your children* depend on it.

Sometimes, even with these steps, it is difficult to see your own personal pattern of depression. If this is the case for you, consider doing the following exercise as a means to assess your need for professional help.

---

**Something You Can Do #12**
*Overcome Resistance to Depression Treatment*

Use a wall calendar, day planner, or notebook. At the end of each day, evaluate that day according to your mood and your interactions with your children (and significant partner, if you have one).

Mark *G* for "good" on the days when you generally have a good sense of well-being, find some things amusing, feel competent, act warmly and affectionately, problem-solve well, or think level-headedly.

Mark *P* for "poor" on the days when you generally feel agitated, discontent, irritable, unmotivated, or down or when you act critically, helplessly, or coldly to your loved ones.

Over the course of a month, notice how many Gs and how many Ps you've marked. If there are more Ps than you think there should be, or if there are just more Ps than Gs, it's time to consider treatment. Show your calendar to the professional you seek out for help.

---

## DEPRESSION TREATMENTS

Comprehensive treatment of depression falls under *four not-to-be-separated categories*: medical, psychological, environmental, and spiritual. Recall from chapter 1 the many influences in the development of childhood depression. They are the same for adult depression. As an adult, you may even be able to look back at your own childhood and discover a host of risk factors that helped make you vulnerable to depression. *Those same risk factors will surely become vulnerabilities for your children if you do not consciously do something different.*

Most formal depression treatments incorporate only some of these four categories. For example, many physicians, after prescribing antidepressants, do not refer patients for psychological treatment. Likewise, some psychologists and therapists do not refer clients for a medical evaluation or address environmental or spiritual issues. My recommendation is that if you are diagnosed with some form of depression and the professional you see does not address all four areas, you should address them. For example, ask your physician for the name of a therapist. If he does not know any or if he says it's not necessary, ask your managed care company, employee assistance program, or local resource center. Resource numbers for finding a therapist are located in the back of this book.

You may be wondering why professionals would discount or disregard some of the influencing factors for depression when it is common knowledge that there are many factors. Again, the answer lies in the concept of *beliefs*. You recall that beliefs shape our attitudes and perspectives about life. Professionals are no different. Very often professionals train in the specialties *they believe* are most helpful for people. They know and can cite the research that validates their perspective and generally treat every person from that model. They may not even consider other models of treatment, depending on how strongly they believe in their own. So a physician might prescribe antidepressants and discount therapy. A therapist may practice a particular form of therapy and discount other types of therapy or medical treatment. A religious or spiritual leader may use a particular form of prayer or ritual and discount all forms of medical and psychological intervention. An herbalist might use herbs and discount prescription medicine. Each professional could give you quite convincing "evidence" for their position.

There is also, of course, the ever-common problem of lack of time. Many professionals are just so busy that they honestly don't have time to research who is competent or not in other fields of expertise. This is so even if they believe in comprehensive treatment.

The bombardment of advertising for antidepressants by for-profit pharmaceutical companies has also shaped how some professionals view the treatment of depression (recall from chapter 1 how media can shape beliefs). I have talked to some therapists who now believe the work they do is secondary treatment because they have been convinced to believe antidepressants work best for *all* depressions and *all* people. If those nonmedical professionals reviewed the available literature, they would discover that even medical and genetic researchers do not put that kind of faith in medication and advise comprehensive treatment.

Following is a review of the four areas of comprehensive depression treatment. Educating yourself about depression treatment will help you overcome your own depression, which, in turn, will help lessen the risk of depression in your children. If your child has been diagnosed with a form of clinical depression, this same comprehensive treatment plan can be adapted for your child. (Depression treatment for children is discussed in chapter 10.) Addressing *all four areas* in your own life models healthy living for your children. It can be compared to the person who has had a heart attack, who then overcomes self-defeating thoughts, stops smoking, eats right, and reduces stress.

### Medical Treatment
Traditional medical treatment of depression usually involves two activities: ruling out other medical problems that may be

causing depressive symptoms and prescribing antidepressant medication when needed. In the past, prescribing medication for psychological problems fell solely on the physician specialist called a psychiatrist. Due mostly to the influence of managed care companies and the epidemic number of individuals now seeking medical treatment for depression, primary care physicians are now commonly prescribing antidepressants.

It is common for a patient to try three to six antidepressants before finding one that is best suited to him. Until genetic research makes this trial-and-error method obsolete, one needs to be patient. It is common to try several kinds of medication for *any* illness, not just for depression. Many of us have tried three or four different kinds of headache medicines before finding the one that works best.

A good question to ask your primary care physician is "Do you consult with a psychiatrist if the first or second antidepressant doesn't work?" Another question is "Are you going to do tests to rule out other problems that may be causing my symptoms?"

Antidepressants help many people who suffer from depression. However, it is important to understand that antidepressants *do not* cure depression. Lifestyle changes are usually also required. As one physician pointed out, a patient taking antidepressants and continuing to live a stressed-out, negative lifestyle is like a person taking high blood pressure medicine, then eating all his meals at fast-food restaurants.

## Psychological Treatment

There are two types of well-researched psychological treatments for depression: cognitive-behavioral therapy and interpersonal therapy.

Cognitive-behavioral therapy teaches a person how specific thoughts influence feelings, which thoughts increase or decrease depressive feelings, and how to change thoughts to reduce depressive feelings. Each cognitive-behavioral therapy session is usually an hour long for a limited span of time (usually six to fifteen weekly or bimonthly sessions). The skills learned in this type of therapy are extremely useful for reducing depressive symptoms and reducing the likelihood of relapse. *In addition, they are skills that can be taught preventively to children.*

There are several good self-help books on the market that teach cognitive-behavioral therapy. I have listed them in the "Resources" section of this book. Be cautioned, however. As helpful as self-help books are, they cannot replace a good therapist. Often, with a book, a person cannot see her own *particular* depression-promoting beliefs and errors in thinking. A cognitive-behavioral therapist specializes in observing and helping people apply the skills to their unique perspective and life situation. In general, self-help books are a good supplement to therapy, not a replacement for therapy.

The second form of psychological treatment for depression is interpersonal therapy. This includes couple's therapy and family therapy. The quality of our closest relationships has a profound impact on the presence of depression in our lives. Repairing and strengthening these relationships has been proven to reduce depressive symptoms. Family therapists are trained to teach social skills, help family members communicate more effectively, and resolve any resentments or difficulties that prevent a comfortable and warm family atmosphere. *Such an atmosphere is vital to the emotional health of children.*

A third form of psychological treatment, for which there is some limited research, is psychodynamic treatment. This method tends to seek underlying and unconscious past causes that influence one's present behaviors. Some people have reported that the personal insights achieved through this endeavor have reduced their depressive symptoms. However, there is very little research backing this claim, and it is recognized that people's memories of past events are colored by their current beliefs. History is reconstructive, depending on present perspective.

It is possible that the intensely personal client-therapist relationship fostered in the psychodynamic method can profoundly effect positive changes in a person, if the therapist tends to create empowering experiences during the sessions. In essence, current beliefs about oneself can be experientially changed, changing the person's view of the past.

In seeking any type of psychological treatment, please heed the following advice: Pay attention if a *persistent increase* in feelings of sadness, anger, resentment, or abandonment occurs *after* therapy has begun. Regardless of any justification, such an occurrence is antitherapeutic. If you don't feel better or at least more hopeful after three or four sessions, consider switching therapists!

## Environmental Treatment

Taking antidepressants and going to therapy are not going to be effective treatments for depression if a person is living a lifestyle of high stress or is in an oppressive environment. Depression, after all, is a disease related to the stress regulatory mechanisms of the brain. Like heart disease, if one is vulnerable to depression, one must examine any environmental factors that may contribute to the development of the disease. A woman living with an abusive husband or a man working on a rotating shift schedule when he is particularly sensitive to sleep disruption is not going to recover from depression simply by taking Prozac and going to "talking therapy."

Most therapists address these situational conditions along with providing therapy. Sometimes a significant other, good friend, church minister, mentor, or sponsor can also be a sounding board to help sort out situational problems and arrive at solutions. Please remember that making changes in lifestyle can not only reduce your depressive symptoms but also *prevent them in your children*. In the next chapter, we will look at specific ways to reduce stress in children's lives.

## Spiritual Treatment

Regardless of a person's religious beliefs, there exists a spiritual side to the treatment of depression. This is a treatment component not often addressed in medical or psychological circles for fear of crossing roles. But there is some evidence that people who live within a spiritual framework seem happier and more fulfilled than people who disregard that aspect of living.

Living spiritually, whether one is an atheist/agnostic or church/synagogue/mosque-going believer, provides meaning and purpose to life. Practices like meditation, prayer, or self-hypnosis create an inner calm and centeredness. Abiding by a universally accepted code of conduct can eliminate reasons for serious guilt and regret. Belonging to a fellowship can reinforce good habits and provide stability and support in difficult times. Finally, practicing charity (almsgiving, volunteer work) creates a personal sense of fulfillment rarely experienced through any other means.

Many professionals have seen countless depressed individuals taking antidepressants, practicing cognitive-behavioral skills, and living in a reasonable environment who remain somewhat depressed simply because they trick themselves into believing that they can live outside of an established set of universal spiritual values.

Martin, age fifty-four, has been in treatment for several months but has only partially recovered from a depressive episode. Fifteen therapy sessions and three antidepressants later, he reveals he has been meeting with a female "friend" who "truly understands" him better than his own wife of thirty years.

Amy, age twenty-three, continues to tell her physician that her medication is not working and requests increased dosages or medication switches. The physician refers her to a therapist who also has no success in alleviating her symptoms. Then one day, Amy discloses to her therapist that she is often "grumpy and bad tempered" at home with her children and wishes the medication would correct the "chemical imbalance." When asked what she does when grumpy, she reluctantly discloses that she yells and slaps her three-year-old in anger and is physically rough with her toddler.

Your answers to questions such as "What is my role as a husband or a mother? What are my values about living out those roles? Are my values realistic? If so, are my actions matching my values?" affect long-term recovery from depression.

Many religious and spiritual frameworks address these issues of conscience. Christians have the Epistle of Saint James in the New Testament of the Bible that exhorts believers to "confess" their faults "to one another." Catholic Christians have the ritual of confessing their faults to a priest. Jewish and Muslim religious frameworks have yearly rituals (Yom Kippur, Ramadan) that help a person evaluate their compliance to a set of values and codes of conduct. Even Alcoholics Anonymous, a nonreligious spiritual program, has the "moral inventory" and the requirement that one share that inventory with "another human being."

Simply stated, living honorably and being frank about

personal failings foster an antidepressant spirit. Living dishonorably, lying to oneself in attempts to justify dishonorable behavior, and keeping unacceptable events secret foster a depressive spirit.

In saying these things, I do not wish to blame the parent who happens to be depressed. Depression is a disease, and simply living right won't automatically prevent every type of depression just as living right won't prevent every type of diabetes or heart disease. But it can prevent *some* kinds of depression. And it can lessen the intensity of depressive symptoms by removing situational factors that cause guilt and shame and by providing hope and community support.

## THE JOYS OF RECOVERY

"Mommy, you chase me," said Peter, age three, as he tugged on my T-shirt.

"Not now, Peter. I'm busy," I snapped.

"Why busy? Don't you want to play with me?" Peter retorted.

I looked at him, my hands covered with dishwater and soap. In the past, I would have pushed him aside, brooding about my own lengthy list of to-dos. But this time his playful face was irresistible to me. "Of course I want to play with you!" I dried my hands and proceeded to play chase.

"What about me?" said Andrew, age six.

"You too," I respond. And off we go chasing, tagging, and giggling until we fall into a tickling heap on the playroom floor.

To play. To enjoy playing. To laugh with your children. This is a wonderful by-product of depression recovery. Just as important, by playing and laughing with your children, you help prevent depression in their young lives. From a biological perspective, the "joy chemicals" are abundantly bathing their little brains.

Recovery from a depressive episode can take a few weeks to several months depending on the severity of symptoms when treatment is sought, which is another reason to seek treatment early or even preventively if only a few symptoms exist. One of the indications that you are truly recovering is your ability to spontaneously laugh and play.

Playing with your children can take several forms. It can be the kind I just described, or it can be quieter, such as playing board games, coloring, or sculpting with clay. It can be playing catch, bike riding, or kite flying. The point is that you find yourself *wholly absorbed in the activity* when you are playing instead of going through the motions while you mentally ruminate about your problems or to-do lists. Children are excellent at knowing the difference. My youngest used to take my face in his little hands and say, "Mommy, you play with ME." If I continued to be preoccupied, he would say, "No, Mommy, look at ME."

Responding positively to these kinds of cues from your children can hasten your own recovery and create a protective atmosphere in your home. By forcing yourself, little by little, to refocus your attention *outside yourself* and your preoccupations, you model the skill of emotional flexibility for your children. Later in this book, I will discuss that very skill as critical to making your child more depression resistant.

After you have sought treatment for your own depression and feel you are making progress, consider the following activity as a means to train yourself to refocus your attention on your children through play.

Practicing playing with your children and refocusing your

---

### Something You Can Do #13
#### *Practice Playing*

Observe your children at play for two weeks. Jot down activities they seem to enjoy and do often. Then try one of the following:

1. Ask your children whether you can join them in an activity they are already doing. For example: coloring, tinkering with Legos or Kinex, or playing a board game. Notice their interactions with you during the time you are engaged in the activity and after the playing is over. Remember, criticisms or controlling behaviors on your part will ruin the play.

2. Suggest an activity. For example: "Let's ride our bikes around the block" or "Do you want to play Uno?" If they say no and propose a different activity, tell them that sounds like fun too, and do it.

3. Say yes once in a while when your children ask you to play, even if it's not an activity you enjoy. This form of self-sacrifice is easier if you use the time to observe your children at play, converse with them about their day, and mentally try to learn something new about them.

---

attention on them helps you heal and helps them become emotionally stronger.

### RELAPSE PREVENTION

It would be a lie to believe that once you fully recover from an episode of depression, you are free and clear. Depression does not work that way. It is a *cyclical disease*. This means that once you or your child has experienced the illness, there is a good chance you or your child could experience it again. *This is why relapse prevention is vitally important.* Managing your life well becomes the key to prevention. By managing your own life, keeping in mind the four areas as you do so, you model self-management for your children. As they model you, they reduce their own risk for the disease or recurrence of the disease.

> Bridget, age eight, has just done poorly on her spelling test. She instantly thinks, *Dad will be mad. I can't show him.*
> Then she recalls a recent event. Her brother Tom, age ten, had brought home a bad grade on his math test the week before, and unlike so many other times when their father "blew up," he had only become a little red in the face and said, "Son, what needs to be done here?" Comforted by this thought, Bridget decides to show her father her spelling test.

Bridget has learned *simply by observation* that she can take responsibility for her mistakes and problem-solve a solution. She doesn't fear severe punishment or retribution in the form of yelling or criticisms because her father, once moody, critical, and unpredictable, is now able to manage his own temper.

One way to ensure you don't slip back into a serious depression is to catch depression early. In the section on overcoming resistance, I discussed the need to watch how your behavior affects your loved ones. Once you have completed treatment, household atmosphere and family interactions will have changed for the better. Keep that in mind. The pattern of playing out "old" family scenarios is a red flag that depression may be sneaking in the back door. A pre-emptive strike might include having your physician re-evaluate your medication, returning to a therapist for two or three "booster sessions," reducing stress, getting more sleep, re-instituting a healthy habit (such as better diet or exercise), or re-examining your values and how you are conducting your life in accordance with those values.

Relapse prevention for depression is a *lifelong* practice. That may seem discouraging, but it need not be. It simply means that once you are enjoying life, you have the right to continue to do so. Simply *be aware* of subtle negative changes that may occur in your body, your thought process, your environment, or your relationships with your loved ones. If they do occur, take action. Otherwise, play!

### SUMMARY

- Children of depressed parents have a 41 to 77 percent chance of experiencing depression or some other psychiatric disturbance or behavioral problem.
- Parents can unconsciously pass on depression-encouraging ways of thinking and living if they do not seek help for their own depression *and* change punitive or critical parenting styles.
- Resistance to depression treatment is common and can be overcome, especially since overcoming that resistance can have such a positive and depression-preventive effect on children.
- Depression treatment needs to include four areas in order to be comprehensive: medical, psychological, environmental, and spiritual.
- When one has recovered from depression, it is important to stay alert for warning signs that depression may be returning. One useful way to keep vigilant is to pay attention to children's reactions to parental behaviors.

# CHAPTER 6

==========

## TEACHING CRITICAL
## THINKING SKILLS: MIND

When children are taught that life doesn't "just happen," but that each choice yields a consequence, they are starting to learn critical thinking.

—MICHAEL D. YAPKO, *HAND ME DOWN BLUES*

When therapists advise parents not to criticize their children, the word *criticize* often takes on a negative connotation. To criticize means not only "to stress the faults of" but also "to consider the merits and demerits of, and judge accordingly: evaluate."[1]

Teaching children how to evaluate what is going on around them and inside them so that they can make good choices is a frontline defense against depression—in childhood, adolescence, and even adulthood. The skills that form the basis for this ability to evaluate are called *critical thinking skills*. When we praise a child by saying, "Now you're using your head," we are referring to that child's ability to evaluate or think critically.

Critical thinking skills, as used here, are drawn from the works of Dennis Greenberger, Ph.D., Christine Padesky, Ph.D., and Michael D. Yapko, Ph.D. They include

1. recognizing the difference between a thought, feeling, and situation[2]
2. recognizing the difference between a fact, a possibility, and an unanswerable question[3]
3. recognizing the difference between fantasy and reality
4. understanding that one choice eliminates another choice
5. developing the ability to look at potential future consequences of choices (foresight)[4]

At first glance, these may seem like very simple skills that most parents have and teach their children. But my experience in classrooms, on playgrounds, at team sporting events, and in my therapy office attests otherwise.

When teachers suddenly load children down with last-minute major school assignments in May after spending a relatively slow January through April—is that foresight?

When a child's coach throws a temper tantrum and engages in name-calling on the soccer field over a referee call—is that dealing well with reality versus fantasy?

When a parent enrolls a child in any and all extracurricular activities desired—is that teaching the child that one choice eliminates another choice?

Critical thinking skills need to be *modeled* and taught.

### DISASTER

Allowing a child to grow up without critical thinking skills is like not putting a helmet on him during a football scrimmage.

And life can feel like a football scrimmage sometimes. If a child isn't taught these skills, disaster awaits. Consider Jacob:

> At ten, Jacob is a model student, is a proficient violin player, is a key basketball player, and has more badges on his Boy Scout uniform than any kid in his pack.
>
> One day, after several hours of frantic searching by parents, neighbors, and the local police, Jacob is found sitting all alone by a wooded stream, crying, "I can't take it anymore. I hate my life."

Jacob was not taught that one choice eliminates another choice. He was not taught to think ahead about what might happen as a result of committing to so many demanding extracurricular activities. He had no realistic knowledge of his personal limitations but began to live out a superhuman ideal. Chances are, when problems with his schedule began to take their toll, he didn't notice his feelings or his body's signals for stress. The result? Helplessness, hopelessness, and subsequent depression.

The inability to foresee the problems and stresses with overcommitment can put a child on the path toward depression. Too much chronic stress causes a chronic release of stress chemicals into the body. Over time, depression can result from this chronic chemical imbalance if the child is vulnerable due to the presence of risk factors such as genetics. So, before your child needs medication for a full-blown depressive episode (or for anxiety, a precursor of depression), you might want to examine his or her schedule and personal response to that schedule.

Some children thrive on lots of activity. Others prefer more quiet and unstructured time. Each child, even in the same household, is unique.

When my son Andrew was in the third grade, his behavior during first and third quarters declined, and he became irritable and easily distracted. When my husband and I questioned him at third quarter, he simply said, "I have no time to play. I have school projects, book reports, homework, and too much soccer." (Yes! In third grade!) When we asked why his behavior was better second quarter while in basketball, he replied, "I love basketball, and besides, you can't play outside in the winter. It gets dark early."

The following year we allowed him to drop out of soccer. His mood and behavior became more positive.

As parents, we can begin teaching our children critical thinking skills at a very young age and continue building on the foundation throughout childhood. The hope is that eventually children begin to internalize these skills so that by late adolescence they are ready to use them independently. Take time to do "Something You Can Do #14." It is designed to help you evaluate and re-adjust the stress level of your child.

More will be said about the importance of unstructured free time in chapter 9. For now, consider the need for free time as a means of reducing the overcommitment that so often builds a pattern of stress and triggers episodes of anxiety and depression in children.

The rest of this chapter focuses on individual skills.

### A SITUATION, A FEELING, A THOUGHT

We must teach our children how to think, not what to think.

—BARBARA COLOROSO

Simply put, if something can be videotaped, it is *a situation*. By contrast, *a feeling* is a personal experience to which we attach one-word descriptions (sad, mad, happy, angry, and so

---

### Something You Can Do #14
#### *Your Child's Stress Level*

First, ask or notice whether your child seems stressed out. Signs of stress include moodiness, irritability, fatigue, stomachaches, and sleep disturbances. If your child is stressed or seems to be very busy, make a list of all your child's daily and weekly activities. A weekly appointment calendar with hourly time slots helps. Include school time, homework time, extracurricular activities, and weekend events. If your child is over seven, have her help you.

Notice whether there is any *daily* free time (car time not included). Block out or highlight that time.

If your school-aged child has very little free time and reports feeling stressed or is showing signs of stress, have a family meeting specifically to discuss how the schedule can be changed and/or what needs to be cut. Aim for a balance between structured activities and free time.

If your child is preschool age or younger, avoid organized activities, except to provide *you* respite (of equal importance, in order to help keep *your* stress level down). Instead, frequent parks, children's museums, open gymnastics, and backyards.

---

on). The older we get, the more complex and diverse the experience of feelings becomes ( "I feel a little sad but relieved at the same time"). *A thought* is anything that is not a feeling or a situation. A thought can include the internal conversation we engage in when faced with situations ( "Why can't she just pick up her room like I asked?" or "Why does it always have to be an argument?"). It can also include words we remember, like "I love you, Mommy." Remembered words usually include the memory of tone, pitch of voice, and style of language. Thoughts also include visual memories and memories related to smell, taste, and touch. An example of remembering with smell would be if a person remembers a parent or grandparent baking homemade bread or cookies at holiday time. Years later, even the thought of the approaching holiday could evoke the experience of smelling the home-made goodies. (How thoughts, emotions, and memories are actually processed in the brain is very complex and beyond the scope of this book. I have included a list of books on the subject in the "Resources" section.)

Thoughts and memories can be very powerful and influential in our lives. That is why, when I talk about preventing depression in children, I emphasize the importance of wording and phrasing things in ways to create pleasant and healthy memories and thought patterns for your children.

To see whether you have a grasp on the difference between a situation, a feeling, and a thought, do the following exercise. It is adapted from a similar exercise found in *Mind Over Mood* by Dennis Greenberger, Ph.D., and Christine Padesky, Ph.D.[5]

### A Situation, a Feeling, a Thought

For each of the statements below, identify whether it is a situation, feeling, or thought. (The answers are listed at the end of the chapter.)

1. Upset                                     _____
2. Sitting in a chair                         _____
3. Talking on the telephone           _____
4. Seeing someone giggle               _____
5. Making a fist                              _____
6. Singing                                      _____
7. Nervous                                     _____

8. "Why don't they listen?"     _____

9. The memory of my child's smiles     _____

10. "This is too hard"     _____

11. Excited     _____

12. "I think I can do this"     _____

13. "I can handle this"     _____

14. Happy     _____

15. "What a lovely gift"     _____

Now that you understand the skill yourself, let's apply it to your children. You can use a similar exercise with your older children or better yet, you can simply guide your children, even younger ones, to understand the differences through daily life experiences.

Jordan, age four, sits in his seat with his arms folded across his chest, face red, and legs kicking back and forth. He has just been told he cannot leave the dinner table without first asking to be excused.

"No, won't do it."

His parents patiently wait the protest out. After Jordan complies, his father says, "Good job, Jordan."

Jordan smiles and sets off to go play, but his father stops him and asks, "How do you feel inside?"

"Happy," replies Jordan after some thought.

"I'm glad for you," says his father. "How did you feel when you were sitting at the table saying no?"

"Mad," says Jordan.

"So you were mad but now you're happy," confirms his father.

This little conversation multiplied with many such conversations helps a young child begin to identify his feelings.

If a child has no words for his experience, give him two or three feeling words to choose from and make your face match each feeling word: "Are you happy (make happy face)? Mad (make mad face)? Sad (make sad face)?" If he chooses one that sounds reasonable, accept the answer. If it is totally incorrect (if Jordan told his father that he was happy when he was red in the face saying no), describe the child's behavior to the child and ask whether the behavior goes with the feeling word he chose.

---

**Something You Can Do #15**
*Identify Feelings and Thoughts*

Here are activities you can do to help children identify their feelings and thoughts:

1. Label your own feelings in front of your children ("I'm feeling excited right now" or "I'm feeling tired today") so that they learn to attach feeling words to behavior by observing you (unconscious learning).

2. Play "Name That Feeling": act out a feeling and have the children guess what it is. The first one to guess correctly acts out the next feeling.

3. Find out whether your elementary school's counseling department provides classes to students about feelings— many schools provide occasional classes on social skills that include identification of feelings. If such a class is scheduled, be informed as to when so that you can reinforce the learning at home.

4. Obtain and use a book or chart describing feelings to young children. The Albert Ellis Institute, listed in the "Resources" section, is a good place to find such material.

---

"Happy? Are people happy when they kick their feet, turn red in the face, cross their arms like this [do it], and say no?"

You want to avoid the habit of telling your child how he feels, because he needs to get to know *himself*. Self-knowledge is a powerful tool.

### A FACT, A POSSIBILITY, AN UNANSWERABLE QUESTION

"The rock floated up and went into my ear," said Peter, age five.
"Is that a fact?" I mused.

Beliefs about reality vary widely. There is very little in life experience that is a fact. Empowering children with the ability to separate facts, possibilities, and unanswerable questions gives them the foundation for the depression-resisting technique of disputing. Disputing, discussed in detail in the next chapter, must begin with the knowledge that there is more than one way of viewing or solving a problem. In the example above, Peter has provided a natural opportunity for me to teach this critical thinking skill at his developmental age level.

I take Peter outside and pick up a small rock, about the size of the one the doctor has just dislodged from his ear. I place it in his hand and ask him to show me how it floats.
Faced with a scientific fact, Peter confesses, "It can't float."
"That's right. Rocks can't float. That's a fact. So tell me, how did that rock get in your ear?"
Peter comes up with about three more scenarios.

I ask him to examine whether each explanation could factually occur.

Truthfully, I never did find out exactly what happened until years later. However, the discussion helped Peter begin to understand the difference between feelings (scared), thoughts ("I'm in big trouble" and "I broke my ear"), and situations (a rock in the ear and a trip to the doctor). In addition, Peter also learned the consequences of poor choices (rocks in ears hurt) and what to consider next time:

"Rocks in any bodily opening might hurt. Best leave them outside the body," I said.

In this case, for good measure, I couldn't help but add a little "good touch, bad touch" lesson.

"Best also to not let other children or adults touch or put anything in any opening in the body: ears, eyes, nose, mouth, penis, and anus."

In order to teach your children the difference between a fact, a possibility, and an unanswerable question, you must first understand the concept yourself. By definition, *a fact* is something that can be proven with scientific evidence. For example, rocks don't float. *An unanswerable question,* on the other hand, cannot be proven or disproven by any scientific knowledge we have to date. For example, you cannot know another person's thoughts at any given moment. Finally, *a possibility* simply means "maybe, maybe not."

Now, do the following exercise to strengthen your ability to clearly differentiate facts, possibilities, and unanswerable questions. The answers are at the end of the chapter.

### A Fact, a Possibility, an Unanswerable Question

For each of the statements below, identify whether it is a fact, a possibility, or an unanswerable question.

1. The number of stars in the universe _____
2. A rock can't float _____
3. Your child has to go to the bathroom *right now* _____
4. God exists _____
5. Your child's age _____
6. Your child's sex (male or female) _____
7. Your child is hungry _____
8. "I cannot achieve my goals" _____
9. The child is a difficult child _____
10. "I'm a bad parent" _____
11. "I'm a good parent" _____
12. The number of grains of sand in the desert _____
13. People can help each other _____
14. People can hurt each other _____
15. The date and circumstances of each person's future death _____

Most things in life are possibilities. The next time you feel discouraged over future prospects, keep this concept in mind.

Meanwhile, remember that it is better to teach your children these concepts through common, everyday events such as I did in the previous example. Teaching with direct experience is much more effective than teaching without it. Below is an activity to help you teach your child the difference between a fact, a possibility, and an unanswerable question.

---

### Something You Can Do #16
#### *A Fact, a Possibility, an Unanswerable Question*

Here are some commonsense ideas to help your children learn the difference between a fact, a possibility, and an unanswerable question:

1. Limit your use of "because I said so." Instead, explain the dangerous facts and/or possibilities to your child. Make sure you are clear which reasons are facts and which reasons are possibilities.
2. Examine your own beliefs about yourself, your children, and even your religion for facts versus possibilities and unanswerable questions. (Hint: All beliefs are possibilities about unanswerable questions. If they were factual, there would be no need to believe.) Decide which of your beliefs uplift your children and which bring them down, which beliefs enhance and which limit their quality of life. Choose beliefs based on this examination, especially beliefs about your children.
3. Play a game with your children similar to the exercise you just completed.

---

## REALITY VERSUS FANTASY

I have been through some terrible things in my life, some of which actually happened.

—MARK TWAIN

Differentiating between reality and fantasy is related to expectations. When a coach throws a tantrum on the field, he is poorly modeling the way to deal with unmet expectations. He may have expected a particular referee call in his fantasy life, but the reality is that another call was made.

Children suffer many disappointments in life, and in essence, most of those disappointments are simply unmet expectations. Teaching children the difference between their fantasy life of expectations and their real life of unpredictability can lay the foundation for depression-free living. It can also make them more aware of how they are influenced by advertisements that play on people's expectations and fantasies, such as certain basketball-shoe ads.

Fantasy, or dreams, can be a terrific foundation for personal achievements. This book is the product of several years of fantasy that eventually became a realistic possibility, shaped by the reality checks of seven publisher rejections, four major rewrites, and the experience of publishing a smaller article.

Fantasy happens *inside* one's mind. Reality happens *outside* one's mind. Depression, you recall, tends to be *internal,* and so it becomes *vital* that children know how to modify their internal fantasy expectations to accommodate external realities— even as they work to make their dreams come true.

Living in reality is actually easier than living in a world of unmet fantasies, broken dreams, and repeated disappointments that are not understood in the light of reality versus fantasy. The following example illustrates how to frame a disappointment in order to teach this critical thinking skill.

> Brittany, who just turned twelve, tells Frances, age ten, that they can't be friends anymore. In Brittany's mind, Frances is still just a kid.
>
> Unfortunately, Brittany's parents agree that the separation should take place, and there is no hope for reconciliation. This is a blow to Frances, who looks up to Brittany and wants to keep the relationship.
>
> Mrs. O'Hara, Frances's mother, takes the time to help Frances work through the disappointment.

"How can this be? How could Brittany do this to me? We were best friends!" Frances sobs. "I've known Brittany since first grade. This *can't* be happening." [fantasy]

Mrs. O'Hara comforts Frances but assures her that sometimes situations change in life. [reality check]

"But can't she see how I feel?" says Frances, still crying.

"I don't know," Mrs. O'Hara replies. "But *the reality is* Brittany has the right to choose her friends. I don't like what she is doing, and I don't like seeing you so hurt by it, but *it is what it is.*"[reality check that honors Frances's feelings]

Frances continues to cry, now positioning herself to be held by her mother. "I don't like it either." [reality accepted]

Mrs. O'Hara then helps Frances remember that she has more than one friend and that, if need be, Mrs. O'Hara will make an extra effort to have Frances's other friends over to the house. "That will not make your loss of Brittany change, but perhaps you can still enjoy your other friends." [still honoring Frances's feelings but begins problem-solving in the face of reality]

Mother and daughter continue to talk for a half hour. Then Mrs. O'Hara offers the family creed, "Throughout your life, Frances, friends will come and go, but your family will stick by you through all the changes. Family stays."

Frances then asks her mother whether she had a similar experience with her friends in her childhood.

"Oh, yes," says Mrs. O'Hara and shares her experience. [validating for Frances that she is not alone in her experience]

Then Mrs. O'Hara uses the opportunity to reinforce the family creed, "Friends come and go. Family stays."

In this case scenario, Frances *expected* that her lifelong friendship with Brittany would last forever. Unfortunately, real life dealt an unexpected blow. Mrs. O'Hara assisted Frances through the disappointment by honoring Frances's perspective and feelings, emphasizing reality, offering realistic options to staying stuck in feelings of loss, and providing a new, more realistic expectation: Family will stay even when friends don't. Mrs. O'Hara also *modeled* that last point by spending time with Frances and helping her work through the disappointment.

To review, expectations are internal fantasy. Reality is what is actually happening. Be sure, as you work with your children, that you yourself understand the difference in your life. The following activity is designed to help you think of your own fantasy expectations as they affect your child's potential for depression.

---

### Something to Think About #4
*Parental Expectations*

All parents have dreams, fantasies, and expectations about their child's future. How specific are your expectations? Is it required that your child carry on the family business, keep up with the family status, or even keep the family name in order to be accepted by you?

What if your child doesn't want the same things or can't achieve what you wish? How will you respond? *How will you adjust your fantasy to match your child's reality?*

Your modeling in this regard is a very powerful, unconscious lesson and can mean the difference between eventual depression or realistic optimism for your child. In the words of an old friend, "Watch your expectations!"

---

More will be said about parental expectations in chapter 9.

## ONE CHOICE ELIMINATES
### ANOTHER CHOICE

You shall know the truth, and the truth shall make you mad.
                                                    —ALDOUS HUXLEY

We live in a country of unlimited choices and a philosophy that shouts, "You can have it all!" In this atmosphere, it is very difficult to teach children that, in real life, one choice usually means another choice is given up.

Countless young couples have come to my office for marital problems following the birth of their first child. Usually, the heart of the problem lies in their belief that they can be parents *and also* be partying, get-up-and-go-whenever-you-want singles. This may work in the short term, but sooner or later (if grandparents don't enable the behavior) the young couple must transition to the next phase of life. You cannot be a parent (however young) and a carefree adolescent (however old). One choice, even if unplanned, eliminates another choice.

At first glance, this critical thinking skill may go against your emotional grain. It should. Our emotions want it all. That's why advertisers play on emotions to get you to buy their products.

Children armed with a solid *experiential* belief that they must make choices, give up what they don't choose, and *enjoy what they do choose* are more likely to choose wisely. They will also be less likely to be overwhelmed by choices. Most important, they will be less likely to think that there is something wrong with *them* because they aren't able to do everything and have everything they want.

You can begin to teach your child that one choice eliminates another choice at a very early age:

"Banana or applesauce," Mr. Kim says to eighteen-month-old Tae, as he shows the toddler each fruit.

When Tae playfully grabs both, Mr. Kim playfully pulls both away, "Not both, banana *or* applesauce."

Tae picks the banana.

Mr. Kim says, "You chose the banana. Good job. Okay, let's say good-bye to the applesauce."

"Bye-bye applesauce," says the eighteen-month-old as she waves bye-bye.

Mr. Kim puts the applesauce away, peels the banana, and gives it to Tae, who eats it.

"Is it good?" asks Mr. Kim.

"Yummy," says Tae.

"Good choice," says Mr. Kim.

A little later in life, some children might not be so compliant with the limits of making choices. They might protest loudly, just as we adults secretly protest loudly inside our heads when we want something badly but can't have it because of other choices we have made. Here is my son Andrew at age five working through choices himself. He had chosen to eat all the Wheat Chex cereal the day before this event took place.

"I want Wheat Chex!"

"We don't have any Wheat Chex. You ate it all up yesterday morning."

"I want Wheat Chex! Get me some!"

"We don't have any."

"Well, go to the store!"

"It's 6:30 A.M. I don't think so, Andrew. How about Wheaties or Cheerios?"

"I want brown cereal!" [Wheat Chex is colored brown]

"Well, Cheerios is brown. Wheaties is brown. Shredded Wheat is brown."

"I want brown cereal with holes!" [referring to Wheat Chex]

"Cheerios has a hole and is brown."

"No, I want lots of holes."

"Corn Chex has lots of holes."

"It's not brown. I want brown with lots of holes!" [that is, Wheat Chex]

"Okay, Andrew, look, we don't have Wheat Chex. You ate it all yesterday. And I am not going to the store right now."

"You don't understand! I really, really want Wheat Chex!" [said in a whining, I'll-die-if-I-don't-have-any voice]

"Well, you can have brown cereal with no holes [Wheaties], or brown cereal with one hole [Cheerios], or yellow cereal with lots of holes [Corn Chex]. Sometimes you can really, really want something really bad and you're just not going to get it. You chose to eat the Wheat Chex yesterday. So now, *you have to find something else to make you happy.*"

[ten minutes later] "Mommy, I'll take some Wheaties *and* Corn Chex *and* granola all mixed together!"

Andrew enjoyed his mix very much. It was the first time he mixed his cereals, so I praised his creativity. Creativity is a strength that, when used well, can help reduce the risk for depression. Also, notice that Andrew's decision took ten minutes. During those ten minutes, he cried, kicked a toy, and then sat in a chair sulking. It is important to give a child *time* to figure out his problems himself. Then have him pick up the toy he kicked and re-request breakfast more politely before he eats.

If children grow up with consistent *experiential* lessons such as these, by the time they are in their preteens, they usually make choices and give up what they don't choose without too much agonizing. Of course, it also helps if the parents practice giving up what they don't choose with some of the same equanimity.

> "I really, really want that new car," says Mr. Hernandez as he looks at a newspaper advertisement. "I can just taste it!"
>
> "Why don't you just get it?" asks twelve-year-old Jesus.
>
> "Because, son, your mother and I *made an agreement* [that is, choice] to save five thousand dollars before we buy a new car so that the car payments will be reasonable for us."
>
> "Heck, dad. They offer deals."
>
> "I know! Oh boy, do I know! It makes it *so tempting,* especially since I want this car *now,*" admits Mr. Hernandez. "But, son, sometimes when you make a commitment, you can't have what you want. Oh well," he says as he closes the newspaper. "Let's go run those errands now.
>
> [he injects humor] "Here I come, old Bessie [the old car], don't quit on me yet!"

If you have mistakenly indulged your children too much, whether for convenience' sake or due to guilt, it's never too late to begin teaching this critical thinking skill. Expect loud protests and grand manipulations, but stay calmly firm. Use yourself and others as an example whenever you can, just as

Mr. Hernandez did for his son. Eventually, your child will learn that one choice eliminates another choice and that you can't have everything.

### FORESIGHT

Vision without action is a daydream. Action without vision is a nightmare.

——JAPANESE PROVERB

Mr. Hernandez's example also demonstrated this last critical thinking skill of foresight. Foresight means being able to look into the future and assess potential negative consequences to choices made in the present. In this case, Mr. Hernandez was avoiding huge car payments that he may not have been able to make with his current income.

---

### Something You Can Do #17
#### *Practice Foresight*

Each time your child needs to make a major choice, such as choosing between two birthday parties on the same day at the same time, have your child *stall the decision for two full days*. During that time, help your child think about future consequences for each potential choice.

Guide your child to make a choice based on this examination, not on just her feelings in the moment. (For example, Tanya's having a swimming-pool party, but Millie is having a simple party. Your child loves to swim, but Millie is your child's best and most faithful friend. How will that friendship be affected by an impulsive choice to do what seems like more fun?)

---

In our now-oriented society, foresight is not practiced very often. The rates of unwanted pregnancies, the spread of the AIDS epidemic, and the number of bankruptcies attest to the inability to make choices based on a knowledge of potential future consequences.

You may wonder what foresight has to do with preventing depression. Depression, as stated in chapter 1, is often triggered by environmental situations. Some situations cannot be avoided, such as the death of a friend to childhood leukemia, but many triggers for childhood, adolescent, and even adult depression are preventable. Foresight provides a defense against impulsive choices that often lead to negative consequences, which can trigger a depressive episode in vulnerable children.

Foresight can be taught throughout childhood with guessing-game questions such as "What will happen if . . . ?" and "What might happen if . . . ?" For example:

- "What might happen if you take that gum out of the store without paying for it?"
- "What will happen if you act bossy to your friend?"
- "What will happen if you don't do your homework?"
- "What might happen if you join soccer and Girl Scouts and try to keep up with your schoolwork?"
- "What will happen if you eat all the Wheat Chex this morning?"
- "What might happen if you start smoking a couple of cigarettes?"

You get the idea. Asking "What if . . . ?" once in a while is a good habit to get into. It is especially useful if your child is about to choose something that will yield a poor result. Feel free to ask your older children "What if . . . ?" about your

dilemmas too as a way to show them that this skill also ap-
plies in adulthood. For example, you can ask your preteen,
"What might happen if we buy this car before we have
enough money to put down on it?"

Thought-through choices are usually good choices. For
children, good choices lead to positive feedback from authority figures and feelings of success. These, in turn, lead to
a healthy self-esteem. Many types of depression are less likely
to affect a child who is realistically confident.

## CONCLUSION

These five critical thinking skills are best taught in the context of everyday life—throughout a child's life. They also
need to be modeled by parents so that children will learn
them unconsciously.

If you are a parent who has struggled with depression, you
may find that practicing these very skills yourself may lessen
the intensity of your depressive moods. This being the case,
you will readily see the value of raising your child with these
skills. It's harder for adults to learn and practice them than it
is for children to grow up with them as a natural part of life.

## SUMMARY

- Critical thinking skills are the frontline defense
  against depression.
- The five critical thinking skills are
  1. recognizing the difference between a thought, a
     feeling, and a situation
  2. recognizing the difference between a fact, a
     possibility, and an unanswerable question

3. recognizing the difference between fantasy and reality
4. understanding that one choice eliminates another choice
5. developing the ability to look at potential future consequences of choices (foresight)

- The critical thinking skills are best taught to children in the context of everyday life. Use the "heat of the moment" as an opportunity to teach a skill. Over time, with repetition, this is the best and easiest way for children to learn.

## Answers to "A Situation, a Feeling, a Thought" (pages 100–101)

1. Feeling
2. Situation
3. Situation
4. Situation
5. Situation
6. Situation
7. Feeling
8. Thought
9. Thought
10. Thought
11. Feeling
12. Thought
13. Thought
14. Feeling
15. Thought

**Answers to "A Fact, a Possibility, an Unanswerable Question" (page 105)**

1. Unanswerable question
2. Fact
3. Possibility
4. Possibility and unanswerable question
5. Fact
6. Fact
7. Possibility
8. Possibility
9. Possibility
10. Possibility
11. Possibility
12. Unanswerable question
13. Fact
14. Fact
15. Unanswerable question

# CHAPTER 7

## ENCOURAGING EMOTIONAL FLEXIBILITY: BODY

Keep your face to the sunshine and you cannot see the shadows.

—HELEN KELLER

Being able to think critically is useless if one doesn't know when, where, and how to apply the skills. This moment-to-moment application is called emotional flexibility and represents the BODY part of the metaphor. The BODY provides flesh and bones to the MIND and also provides "movement" in and out of life experiences.

Emotional flexibility describes a dance of thoughts and counterthoughts, reactions and instant re-assessments of these actions. Like actual dancing, a child will, at first, struggle to know what she thinks and feels and what course of action to take when confronted with situations in the heat of the moment. With *practice*, this flexibility of thought becomes as routine as pausing whenever an emotional moment occurs and asking, "What are my options here?" and, "What's another possibility?" Eventually, a grace of movement replaces awkward step-by-step analysis. Children begin to handle their emotions and manage their conduct. In doing so, they gain self-confidence and self-respect.

## REALITY OR INTERPRETATION

Psychology uses the term *cognitive dissonance*. It describes the tendency of people to create explanations about events according to their personal beliefs. An example would be if a young person dies in a mountain-climbing accident. Family members might explain the man's death as a tragedy, a stupid mistake, a park oversight for not warning the young man of potential dangers, or the will of God. The event—the death of a young man in a climbing accident—is the same. The explanation as to *why* the event happened differs from family member to family member.

In chapter 5, I provided examples of thoughts that parents can have if they explain their life situations through depressive beliefs. I also explained how professionals can interpret what they see only through the eyes of their specific training. These are also examples of cognitive dissonance.

Children, too, experience cognitive dissonance. And it becomes the duty of parents to pay attention to *how* their children interpret the causes of events and provide skills to help prevent a habit of pessimistically or negatively interpreting events. *Remember, the habit of pessimistically interpreting life events is a risk factor for depression.*

To help you recognize some negative patterns of children explaining life events, consider the following statements:

- "I can't do this."
- "I'm too fat."
- "They never want to play with me."

---

**Something You Can Do #18**
*Explore Other Perspectives*

Choose a recent event from a news release, your child's school, or your child's life.

On a piece of paper, write your explanation about why the event took place. Then ask your child for her explanation about why the event took place.

Compare your answer to your child's. Are they the same or different? Did either of you come up with more than one possible explanation?

Interview three other people and ask them why they thought the event took place. Discuss similarities or differences with your child.

Conclude by affirming that the many beliefs about why things happen are simply a matter of perspective.

---

- "I never get what I want."
- "My life is ruined."
- "School sucks."
- "Nobody cares."
- "I'm no good."
- "That's me, born loser."

You should recognize these as pessimistic thoughts even though they are often expressing feelings.

As stated in chapter 5, if you yourself tend to have a self-defeating or pessimistic style, your children will likely have a similar style and therefore be at risk for depression. If such a thought provokes guilt, take comfort in the following activity.

---

### Something to Think About #5
#### *Being Honest without Guilt*

Most parents are loathe to think they may be harming their children in any way. Making a child more vulnerable to depression is something no parent would willingly do. Yet the research evidence is very clear that this passing down of depression-promoting thinking habits from parent to child occurs regularly.[1]

It is important, especially if you tend toward depression yourself, to take action that will help counter this passing down of negative thinking habits.

Instead of denying your ability to badly influence your child ("It's all in the genes"), being honest ("I have some bad habits to work on") can be a freeing experience for you and your child. Once you know *how* to change your habits and teach your child new habits, guilt over past mistakes will subside. The future begins now.

---

## THE ABCs OF INTERPRETATION

Men are not disturbed by things, but by the views which they take of them.

—EPICTETUS

In the 1950s, Albert Ellis, Ph.D., fathered the psychology of encouraging emotional flexibility. He called it the ABC Theory of Emotional Disturbance and Therapy.[2]

The ABC formula makes the concept easy to remember.

| | | |
|---|---|---|
| **A** | Activating event | (Situation) |
| | | *leads to* |
| **B** | Belief | (Thoughts reflecting beliefs) |
| | | *leads to* |
| **C** | Consequences | (Feelings and actions) |

The activating event represents a situation that occurs in a person's life. The situation activates a person's beliefs, which are expressed through thoughts. The thoughts, in turn, influence a person's feelings and actions. Below is the case of Nancy, which describes how this formula works:

> Nancy, age twelve, has just been told she isn't needed for a part in the class play. Instead, she can make and set up props. [activating event/situation]
>
> "I never get the good parts. I'm always behind the scenes. Unknown. Unwanted. That's my life." [thoughts reflecting beliefs]
>
> Nancy feels sad, rejected, and hopeless. She tries to act pleasantly but avoids eye contact and speaks only when spoken to. [consequences/feelings and actions]

As you can see, thoughts that express beliefs about a situation affect both mood and behavior.

Dr. Ellis provided a way out of the dilemma of destructive thoughts. He called this method *disputation,* and added this into his formula:

| | | |
|---|---|---|
| **A** | Activating event | (Situation) |
| | | *leads to* |
| **B** | Belief | (Thoughts reflecting beliefs) |
| | | *leads to* |
| **C** | Consequences | (Feelings and actions) |
| | | *leads to* |
| **D** | Disputation | (Internal dialogue) |

Disputing is not simply arguing with yourself ("No I can't. Yes I can."), nor is it pumping yourself up with empty words ("I am special. I'm great. They don't realize what they're missing!"). Rather, it is a method of *looking at evidence* and coming up with *reasonable* explanations for events. For

Nancy, a good disputation would be the following internal dialogue:

> *I'm not always behind the scenes. Last year I had a part in the school play. Just because I'm not on stage doesn't mean I'm not wanted. What would happen if nobody made props? [Nancy giggles at the thought of a totally bare stage] And if I'm unknown and unwanted, then so must be Ben, Georgia, Ellen, and Frank, because they are also working on props.* [disputation #1]

Another disputation might revolve around Nancy's desire to perform:

> *Okay, what is it that made the teacher put me on the back burner? Does she think I'm not good enough at acting? Then again, maybe she has her pets. Or maybe she just doesn't know how badly I want to act. I think I'll ask her what I need to do to get a part next time.* [reality check, disputation #2]

These are two examples of disputing. In the first example, Nancy uses facts and evidence to dispute. In the second, she uses a "What's another possibility?" method along with a plan to check out her hypotheses.

Disputing, if done correctly, leads to better feelings and more realistic action. It is a technique widely used in both cognitive and rational-emotive therapies and is the subject of many self-help books. A sampling of these books as well as the Web site for the Albert Ellis Institute is listed in the "Resources" section.

---

**Something You Can Do #19**
*Possibilities*

Begin to listen carefully to your child's spontaneous explanations for the "whys" of events.

Notice whether her explanations make her feel good about herself or poorly about herself.

If her explanation makes her feel poorly ( "Nobody wants to play with me *because I'm a geek*"), simply ask, "What's another possibility?" or say, "Well, that's one way to look at it. What's another way to look at it?"

Assist your child in finding explanations that make her feel good without putting someone else down in the process. Use realistic evidence to counter exaggerations.

---

### EXPLANATORY STYLE

In terms of reducing your child's risk for depression or relapse of depression, there now exists a simple modification of the ABC model that addresses the particular style of beliefs children at risk for depression tend to have. The model is the subject of *The Optimistic Child*.[3]

Simply described, a child prone to depression will tend to explain bad events as lasting forever (permanent), as affecting every aspect of life (pervasive), and as having something specifically to do with him (personal). Conversely, he will interpret good events as temporary, specific to a momentary life event, and having to do with something outside himself (nonpersonal). The following examples illustrate the concept.

Tony gets a D on his math test. [bad event]
He thinks, *I'll never pass this course. No matter how hard I study, I always get bad grades. I'm just no good at math.*

First, for Tony to think that he will "never pass" and "always get bad grades" is assuming this pattern will go on forever (permanent). Obviously, there are things that can be done to improve his overall grade. Second, for him to think that he will "never pass this course" generalizes one bad grade to an entire school year (pervasive). Finally, for him to conclude he is simply "no good at math" assumes that the core of the problem is a matter of talent or inherent ability (personal) rather than a matter of study habits.

Hand in hand with this pattern of thought is the opposite pattern when good events occur.

Suzy just received an A on the same math test. [good event]
She thinks, *Lucky break. At least I won't flunk. The teacher must have graded it on a curve.*

Suzy explains her success as an odd stroke of luck (temporary) that is certainly not reflective of a permanent path of success in math. She doesn't view the A as a general state of her grade potential, but as an oddity (specific to a momentary event). Finally, she attributes her success to grading on a curve (nonpersonal). In essence, she is discrediting herself.

These coexisting habits of thought for good and bad events are reflective of depression-promoting beliefs. The research is so clear on this matter that most paper-pencil assessment tools found in physician offices contain questions that assess for this pessimism!

---

### Something You Can Do #20
*Listen for Explanatory Style*

As you listen to your child's explanations for events, listen for his or her explanatory style. Use the chart provided to help you discern key words your child may use that indicate a particular style. Key words are in quotes.

Whenever you discover pessimism, ask your child whether there is another possible reason for the events. If subsequent explanations are also pessimistic, offer optimistic ones (temporary, specific, or nonpersonal explanations for bad events; permanent, pervasive, and personal explanations for good events).

**Permanent**

"forever"

unchangeable

"always"

"never"

**Temporary**

"for now"

changeable

"sometimes" or "mostly"

"sometimes" or "rarely"

**Pervasive**

general/global statements

affects the whole situation

"all"

"everything"

"none"

"nothing"

**Specific**

specific statements

affects just this situation

"some"

"something"

"some"

"this thing"

**Personal**

Because of me alone

**Nonpersonal**

Because of things
other than me

Remember that the key to learning how to change explanatory style through disputing is *practice.* Consider the above exercise as something you can teach your children *throughout childhood,* by example and by repeatedly coaching them to come up with optimistic alternatives to any pessimistic thoughts they express.

### TEACHING YOUR CHILDREN WELL

Remember that children internalize parental modeling and parenting style. Parental criticism that is permanent, pervasive, and personal for bad events and temporary, specific, and nonpersonal for good events influences a depression-promoting belief pattern in the child. A pattern of pessimistic adult criticism has been statistically correlated with children's pessimism and risk for depression.[4] It is important, therefore, to watch how you discipline your children.

The following chart shows you Tony's and Suzy's automatic depression-promoting thoughts/beliefs with corresponding adult reactions.

| Child's Thought | Parental Criticism |
|---|---|
| *Bad Event* | *Bad Event* |
| "I'll never pass this course." | "With grades like that, you'll never make it in life!" |
| "I always get bad grades." | "When will you shape up?" (*Never* is implied.) |
| "I'm just no good at math." | "Well, I wasn't good at math either." |
| *Good Event* | *Good Event* |
| "Lucky break." | "You got lucky." |
| "At least I won't flunk." | "It's about time." |
| "The teacher must have graded it on a curve." | "Girls tend to be bad at math; I'm surprised." |

Now, take a look at what happens to Tony and Suzy when parents correct them with education in mind. In addition to the skills and principles mentioned in chapters 4 and 6, educational correction tends to be temporary, specific, and nonpersonal for bad events and permanent, pervasive, and personal for good events. Below is an example of the same math test event with an optimistic response from Tony.

Tony receives a D on his test.
   He thinks, *I better try harder or I won't pass.*

This simple reaction reflects a belief that a D on one test is not a permanent pattern of failure, but rather a temporary and specific state that will pass if Tony tries harder. Tony is also reflecting the belief that the problem is not because of inherent ability or lack of talent, but rather because of poor study habits (nonpersonal). The resulting feelings for Tony might be disappointment and frustration, but not hopelessness and helplessness.

Here are Tony's parents' likely interpretations:

| Child's Thought | Parental Education |
|---|---|
| "I better try harder or I won't pass." | "There's a problem with this grade. What happened?" |
| | "Did you study?" |
| | "How much effort did you put into it, son?" |
| | "Let's make a plan to ensure better study habits next time." |

Now let's take a look at Suzy's optimistic response:

Suzy receives an A on a math test.
   She thinks, *YES! I'm good! I did it!*

By this reaction, Suzy takes full credit for her success, credit that is permanent and pervasive ("I'm good!"). She also personalizes the cause ("I did it!") rather than attributing the success to something done by the teacher.

It is good for children to feel good and praise themselves for jobs well done. That action increases their self-esteem. True self-esteem comes only after a struggle and hard work.

Now here are Suzy's parents' corresponding parental comments:

| Child's Thought | Parental Education |
|---|---|
| "YES! I'm good! I did it!" | "Good for *you!*" |
| | "Good job!" |
| | "*You* studied hard, didn't *you!*" |
| | "*You* should be proud of *yourself* for all that hard work!" |

Here is a summary chart to help you remember this concept of pessimistic versus optimistic thinking. Remember, optimism and pessimism describe ways to interpret causes of events. How you discipline your child can make a difference in terms of their vulnerability for depression.

| Pessimistic | Optimistic |
|---|---|
| *Bad Event* | *Bad Event* |
| Permanent | Temporary |
| Pervasive (generalized) | Specific |
| Personal (about me) | Nonpersonal (about something else) |
| | |
| *Good Event* | *Good Event* |
| Temporary | Permanent |
| Specific | Pervasive (generalized) |
| Nonpersonal | Personal (about me) |
| (about something else) | |

If you are interested in learning more about explanatory style, there are several books and research articles out on the subject. They are listed at Dr. Martin E. P. Seligman's Web site, found in the "Resources" section.


MODELING OPTIMISM

It is not fair to ask of others what you are not willing to do yourself.

—ELEANOR ROOSEVELT


Practicing optimism and disputing yourself is a requirement if you wish to teach your children these protective skills. If the first words out of your mouth are pessimistic, self-correct (that is, dispute) in front of your children (yes, talk out loud). An example comes from my own home.

> I had just received my seventh rejection notice from a publishing company for my book proposal. I automatically mumbled, "I'll *never* get a book published. It's too much work. I just *can't* be a mom, have a job, and write a book too."
>
> My son asks, "What are you talking about?"
>
> I self-correct, "Well, I just got another rejection notice for my book proposal. *Sometimes* I feel I'll never get this book published [honors knee-jerk feeling]. But I know that's not true. Some authors get twenty or thirty rejections before they get published [evidence]. I'll just have to rewrite the proposal and send it somewhere else." I sigh, "This will just take a little longer than I hoped, that's all. Just got to keep plugging away [disputation]."
>
> "Go for it, Mom!" replies my son.

Perhaps one of the best examples of how parental self-correction can influence a child's beliefs was portrayed in the movie *The Rookie*. Based on a true story, Jim Morris, a baseball player who never made it to the pros in his youth, is convinced by his high school baseball team to try out for the minor leagues at the age of thirty-five. He makes the minor league team but then struggles with his beliefs about success and failure. He almost quits while still in the minors. He doesn't, however, thanks to his supportive wife, who reminds him that quitting would not be a good example for their eight-year-old son. A few days later, he is called up to play with the pros. His hard work pays off, and he realizes his better-late-than-never dream.

The movie beautifully describes how a parent can be motivated to overcome his own pessimism through his awareness that a *change in him will create hope for his child*. In the end, both the child and the parent are changed and can celebrate the hard-earned success.

### CONCLUSION

Learning how to monitor and dispute automatic pessimistic thoughts is a tool that has been proven effective for reducing depressive symptoms in both children and adults. Hundreds of efficacy studies support this method. Teaching disputing techniques to your child preventively certainly can't hurt and will most likely help your child if she has other risk factors for depression. It is worth your time and effort to train yourself in disputation through self-help books or therapy with a cognitive therapist. Self-help books are listed in the "Resources" section.

## SUMMARY

- Encouraging emotional flexibility (BODY) helps protect children from depression.
- Cognitive dissonance describes the tendency to explain events according to personal beliefs.
- The ABC Theory of Emotional Disturbance and Therapy describes how beliefs can influence moods and behaviors and how disputing with evidence can offset negative beliefs.
- Pessimism is a particular style of interpreting or explaining events negatively and is a risk factor for depression.
- A pessimistic explanatory style interprets bad events as permanent, pervasive, and personal and interprets good events as temporary, specific, and nonpersonal.
- An optimistic explanatory style interprets bad events as temporary, specific, and nonpersonal and interprets good events as permanent, pervasive, and personal.
- Parents can teach their children disputing techniques and optimism through modeling, parenting with optimism, and coaching.

# CHAPTER 8

## DEVELOPING SOCIAL SKILLS: HEART

They have to deal with humans all their life.

—AN ANONYMOUS PARENT

Latisha, a twelve-year-old, was referred to my office by her primary care physician for depressive symptoms and social anxiety. Her symptoms had existed for three months. They were mild and had coincided with the start of middle school. Her physician had decided to hold off on prescribing antidepressants until Latisha had attended some therapy.

Her mother reported that Latisha was a frequent recipient of teasing because of her Twiggy-like frame and slight speech impediment.

Latisha seemed shy. She politely answered my questions but offered nothing more. She had two friends at school, who, like her, were outcasts from the mainstream social cliques of her middle school.

Latisha was preoccupied with wanting to be accepted by an established group of peers. She referred to one popular group of girls (the ones who teased her) as "strong" while viewing herself as "weak." Consequently, she kept to herself and perpetuated her isolation.

During the course of the assessment, I discovered that Latisha had a great love for animals and wanted to be an animal conservationist someday. She read books, volunteered at a local animal shelter, and was quite knowledgeable about the animal kingdom.

Intervention became very simple. I just redescribed her view of her social plight in terms of the animal kingdom. The popular group of girls was like a lion pack. She and the other two outcasts were like gazelles. Then came the challenge to her current self-defeating beliefs:

> In real life, gazelles are actually smarter than lions. They know when to stay away from hungry lions and when they can graze peacefully right alongside them. Lions, by contrast, only know when they are hungry.

I instructed Latisha to use her very smart brain and watch this group of girls closely. When could she speak to them? When could she mingle side by side as if she were part of that group? When did she need to keep her distance?

In addition to this, I suggested she contact the local 4-H club, where she might find other twelve-year-old animal lovers. After all, the popular group wasn't the only group in town.

Two weeks later, Latisha's depressive symptoms had lifted. Even with a speech impediment, she found times when members of the popular group would actually converse with her (usually when a group member was alone). She also found other times when she needed to stay away (when the group was together as a unit). Discovering this, she felt smart and confident.

She also discovered a national chat box on the Internet designed for children interested in the conservation of animals. This connected her with other animal lovers her own age with whom she could share her interest.

I set two more appointments for Latisha at one-month intervals. Her symptoms did not return. She reported that although her social status at school had not changed, she had acquired friends through the chat box. This boosted her self-esteem tremendously, and her social anxiety diminished because she had finally found an established group where she fit in. This acceptability provided her the courage to interact with new people at her school.

## PEOPLE NEED PEOPLE

Supportive relationships can reduce the risk for depression.[1] They provide a sense of connection and an external validation of personal worth. A good relationship fosters good feelings and also eliminates isolation, which is characteristic of depression. Even when a depressive episode occurs, supportive relationships often lessen the severity of symptoms, speed recovery, and sometimes save a life.

Developing good relationships is made easier when one has good social skills. The metaphor of the HEART represents this important part of depression prevention.

Good social skills are associated with academic achievement, which often leads to good self-esteem and overall success.[2] Conversely, a lack of social skills tends to lead to a negative self-perception, which has been associated with

depression and behavior problems.[3] The evidence is so overwhelming that in 2000, the Florida school system mandated
that manners be taught in kindergarten as a means of starting
off young children on a good footing.[4]

Social skills are now being taught in most elementary and
middle schools. But, as with all skills, they are more effectively
learned when *experienced* and *modeled* within the home environment. This chapter describes six particular social skills: making
friends, empathizing with others, negotiating terms and setting limits, being assertive, taking responsibility for one's actions, and seeing mistakes, not people, as the problem.

---

### Something to Think About #6
*Home Entertainment Considerations*

It is now common for families to have more than one television, computer, stereo, or other form of media entertainment. Many families have a television or an entire private
entertainment complex in each child's bedroom.

Such arrangements encourage isolation of each family
member from the others. It also discourages a natural atmosphere where social skills can be experientially learned.

The daily life of a family is a virtual learning lab for skills
such as sharing, negotiating, taking turns, and empathy. Less
use of media toys means more time to interact, learn skills,
and create close relationships.

Choosing not to use certain media may be inconvenient,
but the investment of time and emotion is much more valu-
able in the long term. Consider board games, eating meals
together (without the television), and taking turns watching
a favorite show so that you can watch television *together.*

## MAKING FRIENDS

Good friends are good for your health.

—IRWIN SARASON

Watching young children on a playground can inform you of a dozen ways that children attempt to make friends. They introduce themselves, quietly position themselves close to another child, play a parallel activity, drag their parents to the play area, or hand a child a toy. Regardless of the method, making friends—even friends that last one hour—builds a foundation for future long-lasting friendships that can become the cornerstone of a support network.

There are several ways parents can assist children in developing the skill of making friends. First, be social. Invite people over, especially people with children the same age as your children. Begin doing this early in your child's life. Even babies benefit from exploring the faces of other babies, especially if they have no siblings. If your child is in day care, still socialize. As a child grows, he models you more than day care providers.

Go to places where you and your child will meet new people. Begin when they are very young. If you are hard-pressed to find a situation like that when your children are young, I recommend going to a tot gymnastics playtime, a church parent-child group, or a parent-child swim class. Some of these types of groups meet on Saturdays to accommodate parents who work out of the home.

When you and your child are in social situations, there is ample opportunity for your child to *gain experience* in making friends. Don't worry about encouraging shy children. Repeated exposure usually does the trick. It is never wise to shelter a sensitive or shy preschooler or, conversely, to pressure

him into making friends in a particular way. Simply provide a
social atmosphere as often as possible and socialize yourself
even as your young one clings to you.

If you yourself have difficulty socializing, socializing with
your child may be a bit difficult. But it is sometimes good to
do what is a little uncomfortable. The benefits for your child
are worth the discomfort.


## EMPATHIZING WITH OTHERS

Empathy is the ability to see events through a perspective *different from your own*. This is one of the most important skills of
the heart. When a child can empathize, she automatically
tends to have more friends and is thought well of by peers and
adults alike. This, in turn, increases her social status, helps her
to fit in, and subsequently, reduces her risk for depression.

Children can demonstrate empathy in the toddler years.
Sometimes, however, the skill seems to disappear in middle
and late childhood if not reinforced and modeled by parents.
Some parents tend to have particular difficulty with empathy.
They tend to be internally focused and/or preoccupied. That
is why "Something You Can Do #5," found in chapter 4, is
so important to practice. Honoring your child's perspective
in situations serves as a model of empathy for your child's
imitation.

In addition to modeling, there are several leading questions you can ask your child that encourage empathy skills
when situations come up:

- How do you think Jessie felt?
- How would you feel if that happened to you?
- Why do you think Bobby did that?

Such questioning during the heat of strong emotions can help quell a temper, silence complaints, and pave the way toward peaceful resolutions. Just remember to ask these questions *after* you have empathized with (that is, honored) your child's feelings and perspective first!

Empathy, consistently practiced, leads to compassion, which on all accounts is a capital virtue.

### NEGOTIATING TERMS AND SETTING LIMITS

John, age seven, comes to his brother. "I'll let you play my Game Boy Advance if you let me use your skateboard."

"No way," Julian, age nine, replies. "Keep your Game Boy."

Negotiating terms and setting limits is an everyday event in the lives of children. Practicing these skills can prevent overwhelming feelings, feelings of powerlessness, and feelings of helplessness—all feelings associated with depression.

A common way children negotiate terms is when they attempt to change their homework time. Many parents set their child's homework time and routinely enforce it. While this method may be easy and keeps life running smoothly, it doesn't provide the child an opportunity to learn proper negotiation skills.

Another method is to expect homework to be done, but allow children to experiment with different homework times and routines. Consider the following example of a negotiating sequence for a nine-year-old.

"Mom, I need a break from school. Can I go out to play for a while and then do my homework?" [child's proposal]

"It's best to get it done now. Then you're free and don't have to worry about it." [parental counterproposal]

"But I'm too tired. I'll do it faster after I've had a break. I get recess in school. I should have one here too." [negotiation]

"Hmmm. How long a break do you want?" [parent honoring child's reasoning]

"An hour or two." [child's negotiation attempt]

"No, I don't think so. Your recesses aren't that long." [firm parental limit setting]

"Okay then. How about a half hour?" [second negotiation attempt; a willing compromise]

"Are you sure you won't have a hard time stopping your playing to do homework?" [parent encouraging child self-reflection]

"No, it's just a break. I'll get my homework done, and then I'll go out again." [child's attitude and plan]

"Okay, let's try it. But if you whine, disappear, or don't willingly come in to do your homework in a half hour, you've blown it, and I will set the time next time." [firm parental limit setting]

"Okay."

Limit setting is crucial to the negotiation process. As a parent, you *must* set limits. Since I am also saying you need to leave your child room for negotiation, the rule of thumb is to think through what is and is not negotiable. In our house, dinnertime is negotiable; bedtime is not negotiable on school nights. Homework time is negotiable; whether or not to do homework is not negotiable. Every parent needs to set his or her own standards according to the needs of his or her particular family.

Sometimes, parents don't set limits very well. They either

set too many rigid limits in order to maintain personal control, or they set too few limits due to lack of energy, overcommitment, or excessive guilt. Many times parents inconsistently go back and forth between both extremes, creating confusion for the child.

Another problem is when parents who are good at setting limits and rules for their children act as if they themselves are above society's or their own rules. They drink beer while they drive. They lie about their child's age to get the cheaper rate at an amusement park, and then they spank their child when she or he lies. They may regularly speed or take their underage children to places they are not, legally, supposed to be. At home, they may eat food in places the children are not allowed to bring food, such as in the bedroom.

Over time, children can easily unconsciously model and adapt this double standard of rules. Curiously, many parents are surprised when their preteen or teenager later ignores or disregards the family rules, breaks a civil law, or simply argues, "You do it!" When this happens, "How many times have I *told* you?" or "I'm the parent, you're the kid!" are not effective parenting tools.

Limit setting and negotiation skills are important for antidepressant reasons. Teaching and modeling how to say no to some activities or negotiate for smaller chunks of commitment in required activities helps children manage their schedules in a healthy manner. Remember, overcommitment can create excessive stress, which can trigger depression in vulnerable children.

Finally, household rules need to change at different developmental stages in childhood. The older a child becomes, the more freedom and responsibility that child needs to manage. So, in addition to being consistent and encouraging in an atmosphere of negotiation, you can use the following activity as an exercise in allowing a child to negotiate for a change in the rules when he or she outgrows them.

---

### Something You Can Do #21
#### *Democracy in Action*

The next time your child accuses you of being unfair because of a particular rule you have set, suggest that he or she do the following:

1. Clearly define the rule opposed.
2. Clearly state the reasons why it is opposed.
3. Provide a new rule along with *clear evidence* that he or she can be responsible with a rule change.
4. If the new rule seems reasonable, give the suggested changes a trial run but reserve the right to go back to the original rule if your child cannot handle the new rule.

---

If you are a parent who has difficulty in this area of flexible rules, negotiations, or reasonable limit-setting, the parenting books listed in the "Resources" section may be of help.

### ASSERTIVENESS

In order for your child to set limits and negotiate in a socially acceptable manner, he must know how to be assertive. Assertiveness is not aggressiveness, and it is not stubborn obstinacy. It is the ability to be clear about personal limits and speak those limits gently but firmly to others. For example:

"I don't feel like playing marbles today," says Jerry.

"Oh, come on! We have a big championship marble game going on," retorts Bobby.

"How about I referee?" suggests Jerry. "I really don't want to play."

"Okay, you referee. Eddie and I will play Nick and George."

Jerry did not yell, pout, leave, or whine. He simply made his wants known and suggested an alternative that was acceptable to his friends. Had Jerry's friends not accepted his proposal, Jerry might have offered to watch the game. If they still pressured him, he might have then simply restated his position and asked for their respect like this:

"I said I didn't want to play. I'm trying to be nice about it. Stop messing with me!"

Of course, if the other boys are incapable of respecting their friend that day, Jerry could leave. Then again, Jerry may change his mind and join in (after all, this is about marbles, not drugs). In any case, Jerry has communicated his desires and limits clearly and respectfully.

Assertiveness training is widely taught in schools and social skills classes. Alone, the skill does not necessarily contribute to reducing a child's risk for depression. But in combination with having good personal boundaries (setting limits), the ability to negotiate, and the ability to empathize, resistance for depression becomes more evident.

As with the other skills, children can learn assertiveness skills unconsciously through personal experience and parental modeling. The following activity is designed to help you examine your own style with your children so that you can provide them positive experiences and model assertiveness skills.

---

### Something to Think About #7
*Passive, Aggressive, or Assertive Correction*

Children learn social skills primarily through direct parental correction and parental modeling. Consider the following methods of correction and modeling. If your patterned style falls under the aggressive or passive column, a change is needed.

#### Types of Correction

| Passive | Aggressive | Assertive |
|---|---|---|
| Throwing your arms up in disgust | Spanking | Talking |
| Grunting, mumbling | Yelling | Explaining calmly |
| Turning away | Making loud noises or gestures | Using quiet tones, slow gestures |
| No physical contact | Physical roughness (yanking, pulling, shoving, pinching) | Physical gentleness and soothing touches |
| Avoiding confrontation | Encouraging confrontation | Dealing with unavoidable confrontation |
| Sulking, weeping, withdrawing | Throwing things, pounding fists, stomping feet | Stating your feelings or position firmly |

---

You will notice that spanking falls under the aggressive category. There is ample research on the negative effects of consistently using spanking as a parenting tool, including its relationship to aggression in children, poor parent-child relationships, and higher rates of poor mental health in children, including depression.[5]

### RESPONSIBILITY

Those who stand for nothing fall for anything.
—ALEXANDER HAMILTON

In a litigious culture where "the blame game" is the order of the day, responsibility is more often preached than practiced. How can taking responsibility for one's choices and actions help protect your child from depression?

Children often blame others for things they are responsible for, simply because they don't want to get in trouble. If left unchecked, the child could develop a bad habit of avoiding punishment by lying rather than taking responsibility for choices and mistakes. Worse, as the child grows up, he can become anxious or sneaky.

Critical and punitive parenting styles can foster this anxiety or sneakiness and are also associated with depression in children.[6] Teaching children how to take responsibility for their actions—so they can feel good about themselves—begins as soon as they begin to lie in order not to get in trouble: age three.

> "Bethany! There are crayon marks all over the sink! What happened?"
>
> "I don't know. I guess the sink filled with water and the crayon floated up and drew on the sink!"

Consider first a critical, punishing style in response to Bethany's lie. Suppose Bethany's mother reacts by getting

angry, accusing Bethany of lying, and spanking her. Has
Bethany learned how to take responsibility for her actions?
No. She has learned to fear authority figures, which might
lead to blind submission without critical thought or, worse,
generalized anxiety or sneaky behaviors.

Now consider a passive response. Bethany's mother sighs
hopelessly and cleans up the mess. What has Bethany learned?
First, she has leaned that there are no natural consequences
for inappropriate behaviors. Second, she has learned that her
behavior causes Mom to be forlorn and *there is nothing she can
do about it* (learned helplessness).

Consider now the teaching approach that has been emphasized throughout this book:

> "Crayons don't draw by themselves. You will have to clean
> it up anyway." [stating fact instead of accusation]

In this case, Bethany is guided to take responsibility for her
actions *in spite of her lie*.

At ages three and four, fantasy and reality are still concep-
tually mixed up for children. There is no need to confront
such lies harshly, but don't ignore them either. Simply teach
the difference between a truth and a lie by not allowing the
unlikely excuse to prevent the child from fixing the problem.

In addition to teaching responsibility, Bethany's mother
also modeled *three* skills: one social skill (firm assertiveness)
and two critical thinking skills (reality versus fantasy and fact
versus possibility).

I cannot emphasize enough the importance of noticing
*your child's response* to your parenting. Cowering or glazed,
detached, or fearful looks indicate a problem in parent-child
communication. Avoidance, defiance, and persistent anger
also indicate a problem. If a child grows up submissive and

obedient *without the ability to critically think*, he or she is at risk for depression and manipulation by not-so-nice adults. If a child grows up defiant, angry, or sneaky, he or she is still at risk for depression, and eventual trouble with the law, by virtue of poor social skills.

If you are depressed or if depression runs in your family, there is a strong likelihood you use a punitive or passive parenting style. If so, you can help reduce your child's risk for depression by *taking responsibility* for your style and working to change it in the interest of changing the future. Remember, perfection is not required—only repeated self-correction.

Human beings are flowers—open and receptive to softly falling dew, closed to violent rain.

—ANTHONY DE MELLO, *AWAKENING*

## PROBLEMS, NOT PEOPLE

Mistakes are easier to accept when they are not personalized. This last social skill can be a freeing experience for parents and a strong antidepressant social skill for children. It is a skill my husband taught me through his example with our children.

If you are old enough to remember the event or if you saw the movie *Apollo 13* starring Tom Hanks, you are familiar with these words of the crew on the ill-fated space capsule: "Houston, we have a problem."

*We have a problem* are glorious antidepressant words! Begin to use them even before your child talks. Instead of "What did *you* do?" or "What's the matter with *you?*" say the following:

- "Nick, there's a problem with your choice."
- "Pairin, you have a problem."

- "Art, we have a problem."
- "Jill, I have a problem with . . ."

Using the word *problem* in a confrontation takes the fear out of the confrontation. It turns difficult situations into something that can be solved rather than reflections of some inherent personal flaw.

When parents repeatedly view *the child* as the problem, the child internalizes (unconsciously) a sense of shame and worthlessness—harbingers of future depression. This is not only true with *telling* children they are a problem but *repeatedly acting* as if they are a problem, without using words. For example:

- Rolling your eyes and sighing in disgust when they inconvenience you.
- Talking to family, friends, or neighbors about how much easier life would be without them.
- Acting bothered when they ramble on about the minute details of fingerboarding.
- Frequently suggesting that they play computer or video games or watch television so that they are out of your hair. Don't kid yourself, they know what you are doing.
- Acting excited and happy when you have time away from them but acting depressed and burdened while with them.

Again, the key here is *repetition*. I have, on occasion, leapt for joy at a parent's night out and, I admit, have rolled my eyes more than once. But I also try to spend time making my eyes light up when I see my children, calling to mind and letting them know all the things I like about them.

Remember, perfection isn't required, only awareness and self-correction.

If children grow up believing that mistakes, not people, are the difficulty when problems arise, their chances of becoming depressed are significantly less than if they believe *themselves* to be the problem.

---

**Something to Think About #8**
*Red Flags for Recurrence of Parental Depression*

If you have experienced depression and have fully recovered, the unhelpful parental words and behaviors I have just described may also be a sign that depression is returning. Remember, depression is an insidious disease that is notorious for sneaking in the back door. Sometimes noticing your behavior with your children can provide a red flag for your own need for booster treatment, *especially if engaging in these behaviors is not typical for you when you feel good*. So work to practice these parenting interventions, but if you find you are not able—due to fatigue, stress, poor moods, or a sense of "what's the use, it's too hard"—it's time to regroup and focus on your own relapse prevention or seek professional help. Most parents love their children and feel a little guilty when they treat their children like problems. *Doing something* about it relieves guilt and makes you feel good again.

---

### CONCLUSION

Helping your child develop good social skills (HEART) goes hand in hand with teaching them critical thinking skills (HEAD) and encouraging emotional flexibility (BODY). All parts work together within a child, protecting her from depression or giving her skills to combat depression should it strike.

But skills are not the *only* line of defense against depression. Children need something more. They need for these skills to become part of their core personality. In the next chapter, I address how to foster an antidepressant core.

### SUMMARY

- Good, supportive relationships reduce the risk for depression, and social skills are the foundation for good relationships.
- Six key antidepressant social skills are
  1. making friends
  2. empathizing with others
  3. negotiating terms and setting limits
  4. being assertive
  5. taking responsibility for one's actions
  6. seeing mistakes, not people, as the problem

# CHAPTER 9

## FOSTERING AN ANTIDEPRESSANT
## CORE: SOUL

Every artist dips his brush in his own soul, and paints his own
nature into his pictures.

—HENRY WARD BUCHER

### CORE BELIEFS

Throughout this book, I have emphasized the importance of
teaching children protective skills through direct experience
and modeling (unconscious learning) in addition to educating them about concepts (conscious learning). One reason
for this emphasis is found in the therapeutic concept of core
beliefs.

The notion of beliefs has been mentioned several times in
this book: beliefs about depression, beliefs about how to treat
depression, depression-promoting beliefs versus depression-
resisting beliefs, and so on.

Core beliefs are *deeply rooted* and *often unconscious* beliefs.
They are usually about one's self-identity and one's relationship with the outside world. Core beliefs emerge through experience and are often only changed with new, more powerful

experiences. If changed, a person may feel as if his or her entire identity has been changed. For example, someone who has lived with a core belief that he is strong might be thrown into a personal crisis if he suffers a heart attack or even depression. Someone with a core belief that she is unlovable might later come to believe that she is lovable after years of living with a consistently loving spouse.

In adults, core beliefs are difficult to identify without first being in the habit of monitoring automatic thoughts and behaviors (see chapter 7). With practice and investigation, *patterns of automatic thoughts* are discovered that lead to the discovery of a core belief. A behavior pattern for persons with a core belief of "I am likable" would be seeking out friends and automatically discounting any rejection experienced in the process. Conversely, a person with a core belief of "I am not likable" might habitually avoid new social situations, fearing rejection that would (in his mind) validate his unconscious painful assumption.

Fostering the development of antidepressant core beliefs in our children is one of the most powerful ways to reduce their risk for depression, increase their chances for early detection, or minimize symptoms should the disease strike. For this reason, it is metaphorically called the SOUL of prevention.

### DEPRESSION-PROMOTING CORE BELIEFS

Like everyone else, your children learn about themselves through *experience*—the experience of events and the experience of personal interactions. Since core beliefs are formed through *repeated* experience, parents can influence their child's developing core beliefs through *day-to-day interactions*.

Chapters 4, 7, and 8 discussed the difference between

using criticism versus education as a means to correct children. Over time, repeated criticism breeds depression-promoting core beliefs in the child. The chart below highlights some typical critical comments and corresponding beliefs children may develop as they try to make sense of why their parents would repeatedly say such things to them. Children tend to believe what a parent tells them even if they defensively say otherwise.

| Parental Criticism | Child's Evolving Core Belief |
| --- | --- |
| "What's the matter with you?" | "I am defective." |
| "Can't you do anything right?" | "I am incompetent." "I am not good enough." |
| "No, no. Don't touch!" | "I am clumsy." |
| "Let me do it. You obviously can't." | "I am helpless." |
| "You're a lost cause." | "I am a hopeless case." |
| "You good-for-nothing!" | "I am worthless." |

As stated, these core beliefs develop over time *through repeated and patterned interactions.* An occasional temper flare-up with critical words on the part of the parent won't create a negative core belief in the child. When such a thing occurs, the parent can apologize, take ownership for the bad temper and poor use of words, and then correct the statement. For example:

> "I lost my temper. I shouldn't have said that about you because it's not true. You are actually very [insert positive trait]. I'm sorry. Please forgive me."

Parents who *repeatedly* criticize their children are often unconsciously acting out how they were treated as children, reflecting their own core beliefs about themselves. They tend to have depression-promoting core beliefs and unwittingly pass on those beliefs to their children. This is one nonbiological way depression is passed on from generation to generation.

Other depression-promoting core beliefs evolve through nonverbal parent-child interactions. Consider the following:

| Parental Interaction | Child's Evolving Core Belief |
|---|---|
| Distant, detached | "I am alone." |
| Lack of warmth and affection | "I am unlovable." |
| Acting as if the child is an inconvenience | "I am unimportant/worthless." |
| Acting as if the child is a burden | "I am burdensome." |

All these depression-promoting core beliefs are acquired and begin to play out in late childhood and adolescence. If not corrected at that time, they may solidify and extend into adulthood.

## CORRECTING YOUR CHILD'S DEPRESSION-PROMOTING BELIEFS

Fortunately, it is never too late. The wonderful thing about children is that they are naturally resilient and pliable. If you have made mistakes because of your upbringing or your own struggles with depression, any change made now will influence the outcome for your child.

Below is a summary of the ways you can change your child's direction if he or she seems to be developing negative core beliefs.

1. Be available and attentive when you are with your child (chapter 4).
2. Use education, not criticism, when correcting your child (chapters 4 through 9).
3. Repeatedly focus on your child's strengths and praise hard-earned successes (chapter 4).
4. Repeatedly take responsibility for criticisms and mistakes, apologize, and self-correct (chapter 7).
5. If you are depressed, seek professional treatment (chapter 5).

When children grow up with these experiences, they tend to develop antidepressant core beliefs such as

- I am good and worthwhile.
- I am competent and capable.
- I can handle life and overcome difficulties.
- I can succeed, achieve, and persevere.
- I am lovable and wanted.

These core beliefs can not only prevent some depressions but also serve as an early warning system for a child, adolescent, or young adult in whom depression strikes because of genetic factors. Here is an example of the latter:

Mr. Michaels, a fifty-two-year-old father of a young college student, arrived at my office for a work-related consultation session.

In passing, Mr. Michaels mentioned that his twenty-year-old son, Karl, had recently called him from college stating that he wasn't feeling right. Apparently, Karl's

moods were up and down and his thoughts were very
negative. When Mr. Michaels asked whether he needed
to bring Karl home, Karl simply replied, "No, I have
already made an appointment with a psychiatrist. I'll call
you after I see him."

Bipolar depression, a *very* genetically influenced disease,
ran rampant in this family. Mr. Michaels had educated Karl
about the disease when Karl was in high school.

About two weeks later, Karl telephoned and informed
Mr. Michaels that he had been placed on medication, was
engaged in brief counseling, and was already feeling
better.

In my office, Mr. Michaels reported feeling proud.
His son had "caught it [bipolar depression] early," before
serious damage occurred.

The reason this young man recognized his symptoms so
early was partially because he *usually* experienced himself as
positive, capable, and even. He, therefore, noticed the internal changes in mood, attitude, and behavior this depressive
episode had created. He felt no embarrassment seeking help
because he *usually* experienced himself as good, worthwhile,
and lovable.

The situation would have been more complex if this
young man had acquired the core beliefs of inadequacy, unworthiness, and/or defectiveness. In that case, he might have
interpreted his moods as more evidence of his core "badness"
rather than symptoms of a genuine disease. Having antidepressant core beliefs makes the disease of depression easier
to diagnose, treat, and recover from.

## OFFSETTING NEGATIVE INFLUENCES

In addition to acquiring core beliefs from parents, children can develop them from repeated experiences with other adults. Teachers, coaches, and church ministers play a significant role in fostering depression-promoting or antidepressant core beliefs.

> Julie, twelve, had wanted to be a physician for as long as she could remember. At four, she played doctor. At eight, she began watching doctor shows on television. At ten, she began reading about the human body and modern medicine.
>
> Julie loved science in elementary school and had always received As on her tests. Her friends and her teachers all knew Julie's ambition and supported her.
>
> Then, as a sixth grader, the first blow to her dreams occurred. Her science teacher, a woman she respected, idealized, and admired, handed her a C for her midterm grade and remarked, "You'll never be a doctor with grades like that."

Parents need to be aware of how other adults are influencing their children. There are many examples of influential adults creating hope for children living in difficult family situations. But there are also plenty of examples of teachers, coaches, and church ministers instilling core beliefs, through words or deeds, of unworthiness, incompetence, and uselessness in the children they are supposed to uplift. Just as parents can pass on self-defeating and depression-promoting beliefs to children, so can other well-intended adults. Consider the following exercise as a means of offsetting potentially negative influences on your child.

## Something You Can Do #22
### *Offset Negative Influences*

First, be aware of the other adults in your child's life. Speak with them. If possible, watch how they interact with your child or a group of children.

Then notice whether the other adults have a pessimistic explanatory style (chapter 7) or are punitive or critical in their teaching/preaching/coaching style.

If your child seems negatively affected by another adult's negative style, point out the style to your child and emphasize that, while she may need to be respectful in return, she need not take the criticisms or negative comments to heart. Of course, if the other adult is blatantly abusive in language or deed, it is your responsibility to intervene to protect your child.

When you point out the other adult's negative style, be sure to separate that adult's style from what the adult might be trying to effect, which is usually positive. A coach might be yelling and accusing your child of being clumsy during a practice (style), but may be trying to motivate your child to sharpen his ability to pass the ball accurately (effect).

Finally, encourage your child to comply with the positive and wholesome effect and ignore the negative style. I have sometimes used the metaphor of water rolling off a duck's back as it swims upstream. But again, if the other adult is excessively or relentlessly critical or abusive, or if your child cannot seem to shake off the discouraging effect of the other adult's style, you need to intervene directly.

OTHER WAYS TO FOSTER A
DEPRESSION-RESISTANT CORE

In addition to fostering positive core beliefs and offsetting negative influences, there are six other ways parents can strengthen the core identity of their child. These are

- accepting the real child
- promoting inner quiet and focusing skills
- promoting unstructured free time
- modeling and teaching self-management
- encouraging the view that one is part of a larger world
- promoting humor and other positive emotions

## Accepting the Real Child

David G. Fassler, M.D., and Lynne S. Dumas, in their book *"Help Me, I'm Sad,"* describe loving and supporting the real child as concentrating less on who and what you would *like* your child to be and more on discovering the unique person your child *really* is.[1]

In chapter 6, I discussed parental expectations versus observing your child's reality. Another way parents sometimes express their expectations (verbally or nonverbally) is by wishing their child had different personality traits. They wish their shy child was more social; their active child, more settled; their strong-willed child, compliant; their talkative child, quiet; their moody child, even tempered; their uncoordinated child, more graceful. These wishes do not help a child develop his natural traits into strengths that will serve him. They also do not help a child accept and sidestep innate personal weaknesses, which we *all* have, as he moves forward in life.

Take a moment to do the following activity. It will help

you clarify your child's actual traits and interests, whether or not they match your wishes for your child.

---

### Something You Can Do #23
#### *Your Child's Traits*

Make a list of your child's physical, emotional, and behavioral traits—good and bad. Now make a list of your child's interests, whether you approve or not. If you have difficulty doing this, spend the next month *observing* your child.

Once the list is complete, write how your child's interests and personality traits may help your child be productive and successful in life. *Include the interests and traits you don't approve of or don't like about your child.*

If you have difficulty with this exercise, enlist the help of others, such as your spouse, grandparent, or your child's teacher.

---

Once you have identified your child's unique traits, you can begin to orchestrate situations where her traits can be best served or circumvented, as the case may be, using the skills and techniques described in this book. Remember, every trait, talent, or interest can be *utilized* in your child's favor (chapter 4). For example, a child who likes making loud noises and banging on things can take carpentry or drum lessons. An intellectual, quiet, and not athletically inclined child might do well joining the chess club or math club.

## Promoting Inner Quiet and Focusing Skills
Wisdom begins with wonder.

—SOCRATES

Prayer, meditation, contemplation, guided imagery, and self-hypnosis are all techniques that promote inner quiet and focusing skills. Some children naturally take to such quiet time. For others, especially children who obsess on negative thoughts or are easily distracted, quiet focusing is much more difficult. In any case, it is still an excellent skill for dealing with a hectic world and staying in touch with a core self.

I once knew a Catholic family who prayed the rosary every night. (The rosary is a prayer form where reciting a series of Our Fathers, Hail Marys, and Gloria Patris creates a mantra while the person praying attends to a scripture passage or doctrinal teaching.) The family had a nine-month-old who was expected to sit on his mother's lap for "one decade" (about three to five minutes). Whenever the child squirmed, the mother would gently redirect his behavior. As the child grew older, his *tolerance for quiet* and his attention span grew. By the age of nine, the child could kneel motionless for five decades (fifteen to twenty minutes). This is a marvelous feat for a nine-year-old.

That family's motivation for praying the rosary was not to promote inner quiet and the ability to focus in the secular sense, but nevertheless, the skills were attained. So, if you belong to a religious tradition, be still and pray.

If you do not belong to a religious tradition, there are other ways to encourage the same skills in your child. With very young children, read to them or tell them stories. This encourages the practice of sitting still and being totally focused on one thing, in this case, the story. Begin with very short stories, and gradually increase the length of the story time. Be sure to animate your voice as you read to make the story interesting for your child.

School-aged children can lie on a couch, bed, or floor or sit on a comfortable chair for two, five, and, eventually, up to ten or fifteen minutes. While lying, have them look at a spot on the wall or ceiling or close their eyes while you instruct them to pay attention to relaxing each part of their body from head to toe (progressive muscle relaxation technique). Describe each point of relaxation one at a time ("Now notice the top of your head, relax your head. Now notice your ears, relax your ears. Now your mouth. Now your neck. Your shoulders," and so on).

Still another way to teach focusing is the three-breaths technique. Have your child sit comfortably and tell her to breathe in and out deeply one time. During that first exhale, emphasize how relaxing it can feel to let out all the busy thoughts or problems. Then instruct your child to concentrate only on her breathing: in and out. She need not change how she breathes, just notice that the air is going in and out. She should do this only three times, especially if she is not used to longer focusing times. Eventually, when she gets the hang of it, she can increase to five breaths and perhaps then graduate to a longer time.

A final, somewhat different method of focusing is drawn from the martial arts and yoga. Karate, judo, aikido, and yoga all require focused attention during movement or body positioning. If your child is not in a martial arts or yoga class, have him pick three to five simple motions to repeat, such as a gentle down motion with his arms, slightly squatting, then gently pushing upward with hands toward the sky. While he repeats the movements, one after another, have your child inhale and exhale in rhythm with the motion. To teach this you will, most likely, need to model the movements and breathing first. This technique is very helpful when teaching active children to focus.

Promoting inner quiet gives children an edge in tense situations. Many of the anxious and depressed children I have treated have used the three-breaths or focused-movement skill to stop scary or pessimistic thoughts, which then can be disputed calmly. The focusing aspect of these techniques has also helped children who are easily distracted.

Even if you have very young children, I recommend spending five minutes a day practicing some form of focusing skill. You can even use massage to help settle down these youngsters. In our house, giving our children soft back rubs with hypnotically voiced suggestions of how pleasant and relaxed they felt was a bedtime ritual for years.

---

### Something You Can Do #24
#### *Practice Focusing Skills*

Obtain and use a book for practicing and teaching children relaxation techniques, hypnosis, or prayer. The public library, your place of worship, or the World Wide Web may be of assistance.

Consider enrolling your child in a martial arts or yoga class. Be careful, especially with martial arts classes, that the teacher emphasizes focus and self-discipline and *not* the glory of combat.

---

## Promoting Unstructured Free Time

One of the most delightful articles I have ever read began with the following:

> As a child, I loved a vacant lot we called "the woods." I went there alone, to read or to wonder. I went there with friends to build tree forts. Sometimes we'd use a magnifying glass to burn ants or to light little tepee fires. Sometimes one of the boys would pee on the fire to put it out, and we'd laugh our heads off.
>
> Our parents knew none of this, of course, but that

was the point. Back then, parents pretty much stayed out
of children's business. Play went mostly unsupervised,
and it was deliciously free form.[2]

The author, Ellen Ruppel Shell, goes on to describe herself hanging out after school and on weekends waiting for
friends to show up. If they didn't, she would bounce a ball,
ride a bike, or play jacks. In any case, *she took responsibility for
her own time.*

By contrast, today's children are in organized sports, dance
lessons, art classes, civic groups, chess clubs, Boy Scouts and
Girl Scouts, ad nauseam. Some barely have time to breathe.

In order for a child to develop a sense of self, *he must have
the freedom to explore and learn about himself and his relationship
with the world.* He must learn that if he stomps on a bee bare-
foot, it might sting him. If he pops a wheelie too high, he might
get a flat tire. If he repeatedly jumps off higher and higher objects in order to prove himself to his seven-year-old peers, his
feet might be bruised the next day. Sure, a parent could tell a
child all this, but then he wouldn't *learn from experience.*

In actuality, "keeping children busy" and always "making
sure they have something to do" can set them up for trouble
*and* possibly depression. When a young child is overscheduled
or constantly entertained, he experiences a life where he
doesn't have to take responsibility for the good use of time.
Experience teaches him that *others* will entertain him and
keep him busy. As a teenager or adult, this core belief ("I must
be entertained") spells trouble. Most forms of livelihood do
*not* entertain. To the contrary, the employee needs to put
meaning into the work in order to derive pleasure from it.

There are other problems with overly structuring children's time. If a child is to develop an antidepressant core,
she must first have a sense that she even *has* a core—a soul—

an essence uniquely hers. She will *not* experience that sense while going from structured activity to structured activity without a breath. She needs time to simply be with herself.

When my son Andrew asked to stop playing soccer, I was a bit nervous about what he would do with his time. That fear became more acute when his two neighborhood friends were not around after school because of their structured activities. My fears were unfounded. During his playtime, he mastered a skateboard, practiced roller hockey, renewed an interest in woodworking, and began listening to music. When he complained he was bored, I offered a job. He usually read a book instead. I allowed computer and Nintendo games at times but was careful they didn't become an easy out for boredom.

---

**Something to Think About #9**
*Motive*

Consider your motive for scheduling or entertaining your child. Is it out of fear that your child will get into trouble if allowed free time? Have you been influenced by articles or tradition? Do you schedule your child because of your ambitions that he or she compete or for the sake of convenience?

Take steps to correct any overscheduling or over-entertaining.

---

In suggesting you provide your child unstructured free time, I am *not* suggesting that you take your child out of *all* structured activities. Involvement in some extracurricular activities is so good for children, measuring its absence or presence is often used to assess for childhood depression. Children who are not involved in structured activities miss out on the vital life experiences of team spirit and group participation that build social skills. But too much structured activity (including television and computer games) can lead to stress, an inability to manage time, and a loss of a sense of self. The key is *balance*.

---

### Something You Can Do #25
### *Unstructured Play*

Here are some tips to help your child learn how to take responsibility for his or her free time:

**Younger Children**
- Have books, Lego/Kinex-type building toys, blocks, art supplies, Play-Doh, chalk, and empty boxes in your house at all times.
- Save old costumes, clothes, ribbons, fabric scraps, and wood pieces.

**Older Children**
- Buy a bike, scooter, skateboard, or in-line skates— secondhand if need be. Remember to purchase a helmet.
- Have a standing offer to pay for special jobs or tasks purposely designed to earn money.
- Have a standing offer to allow for experimental woodworking, meal creating, or gardening projects.
- Make the following items available: musical instruments, books, gardening tools, snow toys, marbles, kites, balls, and so on.

---

Sometimes, unstructured activities will require your participation, such as transporting children to parks, skate parks, ice-skating rinks, snow hills, or beaches. Your children may also want you to come see their creations with building blocks, gardening tools, or wood, or they may want to show you their latest bike stunt. Take the time to cheer them on. This reinforces their creativity. Remember, creativity is an antidepressant skill!

## Modeling and Teaching Self-Management
Those who master others are strong; those who master themselves have true power.

—LAO-TZU

Self-management is the ability to pause long enough to think through an appropriate course of action when the sudden and unexpected strikes. It is the restraint you practice when your child comes home with a bloody nose and swollen eye claiming a classmate beat her up for nothing. And it is also the self-discipline a grade school student practices when he chooses to sit through seemingly tons of homework instead of going out to play on a beautiful autumn day. In the long run, nothing creates a more powerful feeling of self-esteem than the habit of self-management.

The most powerful means of teaching your child how to manage her moods, desires, wants, and thoughts is to *model the behavior*. I realize that sometimes this is not an easy feat, but self-management is a core, essential antidepressant skill.

There are several areas where self-management can be practiced: temper control, choosing to act in spite of strong inhibiting emotions such as fear or anxiety, and choosing not to act when strong emotions encourage action. Try asking yourself and your child these questions when feeling a strong emotion:

1. What are you feeling right now? (scared, angry, lonely, afraid, and so on)

2. What are your feelings telling you to do? (run away, keep silent, do something you shouldn't do, and so on)

3. How will you feel about yourself if you do what your feelings want, right now? (usually relieved in the short term but anxious, remorseful, or bad in the long term)

4. How can you act in a way that doesn't harm yourself or anyone else?

Using these questions as guidelines, you can teach your children the beginnings of self-management. The questions will need to be asked over and over again at every stage in childhood so that they become more routine in adolescence and adulthood.

Honoring and managing moods using self-awareness and the disputing exercises described in chapters 6 and 7 can also be very helpful. With practice, these skills can become the source of great pride and self-esteem, especially if you or your child has already experienced clinical depression.

## Encouraging the View That One Is Part of a Larger World

The miracle is this—the more we share, the more we have.

—LEONARD NIMOY

Like many schools, our children's school has an annual fund-raiser. The fund-raiser requires a year's worth of planning and organizing, weeks of ticket selling, and days of arranging for the assorted food and games.

Every parent is expected to participate. Every student, even kindergartners, are encouraged to do their part for its success. In a very real way, the fund-raiser begins to teach that

---

### Something You Can Do #26
*Self-Management*

Part A:

Pick one area in *your* life where self-management needs to be practiced (temper control, healthy eating habits, using a new parenting skill). Using the four-question framework on pages 169–170, practice managing this one particular area for two months. When you feel comfortable managing this area, move on to a second area.

Part B:

Pick one area in *your child's* life that needs self-management (bathing regularly, consistently doing homework, temper tantrums). Tell your child you are going to help him do better in this particular area. When the situation comes up, ask your child the four questions and guide him to self-management in that area. When your child has mastered an area, list it in the success journal ("Something You Can Do #9") and move on to a second area.

---

there is more to life than immediate wants and ambitions. Interconnectedness exists between self, school, parents, and community.

Encouraging the knowledge that each of us is part of a larger world counters the depressive viewpoint that each of us is an island ("look out for number one" is actually a depression-promoting statement). As discussed in chapter 8, the less the sense of isolation, the more likely depression will not grab hold of your child. Often, being part of the larger world is expressed through volunteerism.

*Volunteerism begins at home.* Expecting your child to do some chores for free simply because working together is part of being a family is the first way to teach this community skill. Adults are not paid for keeping up their living space; neither should children be paid for basic household maintenance. Clean rooms and toys put away are simple considerations that reflect the awareness of being part of a larger group.

Parents can model this interconnectedness by freely donating a little extra time to listening to their child read, helping her with homework, or playing a game with her when she is lonely. Believe it or not, this kind of parental behavior *is* volunteerism, and it does much good.

Community volunteerism occurs at school, in church, in hospitals, or with civic groups. It should always come second to home volunteerism and be engaged in with reasonableness. As often as possible, choose activities where the children can participate or at least be near you. This way, they learn, unconsciously, that it is simply part of life to give up some personal time for charitable work. Of course, when your child is young, make sure your charitable deeds are done in short time frames.

There is an antidepressant quality to charity. You forget yourself and become more mindful of your surroundings. With some mild depressions, this activity has been known to facilitate recovery.

## Promoting Humor and Other Positive Emotions

Live well, laugh often, love much.

—EPITAPH, FATHER RICHARD A. WUERTZ

Seriousness is a harbinger of depression. Laughing is a potent antidepressant. Laughing produces endorphins, brain chemicals that provide the experience of pleasure. The more endorphins, the less depression.

There are children who, for various reasons, don't produce the right combination of brain chemicals to truly feel

---

### Something to Think About #10
#### *Self versus Others*

There is much advice in depression books that the depressed person should take better care of himself or herself. Isn't all this caring for others a setup for becoming overwhelmed or starved for having one's own needs met?

The key is in the limit setting. Living in a community, family included, means *all* members should get *some* of their needs met. This is a balancing act that often requires that no one individual receives all the time.

Too much self-preoccupation and orchestrating to come out on top in the need-fulfillment category will cause resentment from the rest of the members. Too much self-sacrifice on the part of one individual creates resentment and feelings of victimhood in that individual and a sense of entitlement in the other members. Gratifying feelings come only from the balanced *give-and-take*.

---

pleasure. But except in rare instances, children are not *initially* hardwired that way. They naturally derive pleasure from life and they *learn* humor.

If quick wit and "strikes me funny" scenarios are not easily conjured up in your family, perhaps a more action-oriented approach is needed: *play while you work*. Here are some suggestions: a gentle tickling poke or soft back rub when things get too serious, swaying to upbeat music while cooking or cleaning, or imitating the voice tones of your favorite cartoon/sitcom character when giving "orders" to your child.

Good humor and positive emotions can energize your child and, consequently, can provide some protection from depression.[3] Positive emotions can also enhance learning, interest, and involvement.[4] Best of all, they build durable resources that can be tapped long after the positive emotion subsides.[5]

With a foundation of humor and positive emotions, your child will be less likely to use scripted, restricted, and possibly negative methods of solving problems in a crisis. Instead, new ideas and ways to solve problems, even homework problems, may become evident.[6]

The importance of positive emotions as a means of reducing the risk of depression is only now beginning to be researched and made available to the general public. I hope we will soon begin to see the practical application of that research in schools, places of work, and in parent education.[7]

---

### Something You Can Do #27
#### *Promote Humor*

Below is a list of practical ways to promote humor in your home:

- Share jokes found in newspapers, in magazines, and at playgrounds. Avoid jokes that poke fun at various cultures or disabled people, or otherwise reduce the dignity of any person.
- Laugh at your child's jokes, even if they aren't funny or you've heard them before.
- Go to the library and borrow joke books or humorous stories.
- Watch wholesome humor on television. *America's Funniest Home Videos* doesn't qualify since most of these videos are of people getting physically hurt.
- Play party games with your child.
- Do silly things while you complete household tasks, as described on page 173.

---

## Something You Can Do #28
### *Encourage Positive Emotions*

A very good way to encourage positive emotions in your home is to pay particular attention to your child's waking-up and going-to-bed experiences. First thoughts and last thoughts often set the tone for a good day or a restful sleep. Here is a list of suggestions for making your child's first and last experiences of the day more positive.

Waking:

- Awaken your child with gentle music, soft tones of voice, or gentle touches.
- Make a good breakfast.
- If morning motivation is a problem, play motivating music and sing with it while you help your children get ready for school or morning day care. Use positive religious music, nursery rhyme music (for younger children), or a favorite *positive* radio station. If you can imagine the absurdity, we recently used Steppenwolf's "Born to Be Wild" and "Magic Carpet Ride" at 6:00 A.M. The unusualness of the choice made for some humorous mornings!

Sleeping:

- Spend time settling down before you put your children to bed. Read, watch an educational television show *with them*, sing a song or two.
- Recount pleasant things about the day and let your children talk through any bad experiences until they seem to have resolved them and feel better.
- Use soft speech, gentle voices and touches, and slow movements at bedtime.
- Just before they go to sleep, mention one good thing they can anticipate upon awakening. A special breakfast can be a nice thought.

### CONCLUSION

The soul is the very essence of a human being. Fostering an antidepressant core in your child can actually be a growing and positive experience for the parent.

While science hasn't yet "proven" some of these preventive skills of the SOUL, evidence about the development of disease through genetic-environmental interactions *over time* is very clear. We cannot change our children's genes. We can change the environment so that the evolution of gene vulnerability might be modified or the bad consequences of an inherited disease might be minimized.

### SUMMARY

- Core beliefs are deeply rooted, often unconscious beliefs about one's self-identity and one's relationship with the outside world.
- Core beliefs are formed through experiences.
- Core beliefs form in childhood and are modified throughout life.
- The techniques described in this book should be used *throughout childhood* in order to promote antidepressant core beliefs.
- Some ways to foster antidepressant core beliefs are
  1. accepting the real child
  2. promoting inner quiet and focusing skills
  3. promoting unstructured free time
  4. modeling and teaching self-management
  5. encouraging the view that one is part of a larger world
  6. promoting humor and other positive emotions

# CHAPTER 10

## COMMONSENSE DEPRESSION PREVENTION

God, grant me the serenity to accept the things I cannot change,
the courage to change the things I can, and the wisdom to know
the difference.

—REINHOLD NIEBUHR

### DEPRESSION IS A DISEASE

With so many considerations about depression, a parent
could feel overwhelmed and discouraged. Why bother putting forth all this Herculean effort if depression is a biological
illness? Why not simply wait and see whether a child develops the disease? If a depressed parent, why not simply take
medication and get on with life?

The reason is, quite simply, that the research to date indicates that depression is not a purely biological phenomenon.
Many diseases aren't. Not only can some depressions be prevented, but the devastating effects of a bout of depression can
be greatly reduced through early intervention, a strong social
network, and a history of good coping skills.

Keeping this in mind, there are several points that need to

be reviewed in this chapter. First, depression is a medical condition. It is not caused by any one factor, such as bad genes, bad parenting, or a bad environment. Rather, depression's development is influenced by a combination of factors: biological, psychological, and sociological.

Depending on the type of depression, one influential factor may have more weight than others for a given child. Some depressions are more genetically influenced. Others are more environmentally influenced. How risk factors specifically interact to encourage the development of depression is still not known. One child may grow up with few risk factors, then at ten years old, experience a traumatic event that triggers a major depressive episode. Another child may have many risk factors but never develop the disease. A third child may have only one or two risk factors (most children do) and mysteriously develops the illness at age six.

While we can't yet predict individual cases, we can say that the overall rates of depression in children at risk go down with preventive interventions. The important thing to remember is that if your child goes on to develop clinical depression in spite of your efforts, it doesn't mean you have failed. It simply means there are always factors out of a parent's control. If your child succumbs, then the same techniques taught in this book to reduce the risk for depression can complement medical and psychological treatment and later be used to help reduce the risk for relapse.

## EVERY CHILD IS UNIQUE

The second point that needs to be reviewed is that every child is unique. If you have more than one child, you already know this. One child sleeps well; the other child does not. One child reads well; the other does math well. One child is

"Miss Sunshine"; the other is more reserved. No two children are alike even in the same home.

This is vital to remember when you apply some of the interventions in this book. Some children want to be taught, and you can explain to them what you are doing and why. Other children are less interested. For them, you will need to provide the atmosphere and intervene without explanation. Praise them when they inadvertently model your purposeful intervention.

Some children need critical thinking skills more than social skills. Others need the reverse. Still others need only one or two particular skills in each area. Be sure to tailor your interventions to your particular child's needs. If you think she needs help in many areas, pick a couple of areas at a time. After all, you have an entire childhood to teach her, and this book is designed to be used over and over again.

## CHANGE IS GRADUAL

Nothing in the world can take the place of persistence.

—CALVIN COOLIDGE

The third point is that changes in your parenting style and changes in your children take time. There is no need to rush through, do an exercise once or twice, and expect change to occur. Repetition is the mother of learning, after all. True progress has its ups and downs. I have been practicing these principles for several years now. Sometimes I do well. Sometimes I don't. Sometimes I think I'm really helping my children. Other times, I wonder why I try. This is normal. Changes evolve over time. Often you don't see the fruits of your labors until your children are young adults. Think again of that marvelous father whose son detected bipolar depression

in himself before the disease had devastating effects. Sometimes you never see the fruits of your labors. They occur
without your knowledge.

There is a myth that how a child turns out as an adult is
solely based on how that child was parented. This is simply
not true. No parent or child is perfect. Mistakes, poor attitudes, disease, and major problems occur in the vast majority
of people's lives. So, as you persist in your endeavors of parenting, be patient with yourself in low or frustrating times
and remember, "This too shall pass."

### WHAT IF MY CHILD IS DEPRESSED?

It is entirely possible you have picked up this book because
you suspect your child may be depressed already. As I stated
in chapter 2, don't wait. Begin by getting your child assessed
by a medical physician. From there, seek a therapist skilled
and experienced in treating depression in children.

I would like to say that getting treatment for your child is
easy, but I would be misleading you. Today there are many
considerations. First, not all therapists are well trained or
skilled in treating depression in children or adults, even if
they say they are. Second, not all managed care companies
have the most experienced therapists on their panel. Third,
sessions may be limited and reimbursement skimpy. Given
these obstacles, what can you do?

1. *Find a therapist in your area.* Use the discussion on
   treatment in chapter 5 to guide your choice. Make
   sure the therapist has the proper credentials and is licensed by the state. Referral resources and Web sites
   are listed in the "Resources" section of this book.
2. *Ask questions!* Questions to ask managed care compa-

nies and potential therapists are listed in the activity
on page 183.

3. *Be assertive about your child's care.* Understand why a
clinician diagnoses your child in a particular manner.
The clinician should be able to give you specific symptom criteria for a diagnosis. It is not a matter of professional "experience." If your child's therapist cannot
provide specific symptom criteria or is evasive, consider obtaining a second opinion.

4. *Observe your child.* Is medication or therapy making
your child worse, better, or producing no change? Tell
the professional if treatment is not working. Give details. This helps a professional adjust his or her treatment or method. As stated in chapter 1, if you don't
like what is happening, you have the right to switch
professionals.

5. *Report any blatantly condescending, belittling, or abusive
behavior to the appropriate authorities, such as to the licens-
ing board and/or the managed care company.* Professional
guidelines and disciplinary structures are in place in
every legitimate professional organization, which is
why it is important to consult a *licensed* professional.

## TREATMENTS

Children with depression are treated in different ways depending on the severity of the depression. Unless a serious
depression exists, treatment protocol usually recommends
individual cognitive-behavioral therapy, social skills training,
and/or family therapy. You will find that much of the treatment includes more tailored and systematic versions of what
is found in this book.

The advantage of having the services of a good therapist is

that she can individualize protective skills and be more sensitive in addressing the emotional components of your child's particular situation—something no book can do. Even if your child's therapist uses this book to supplement therapy, this book is not meant to be a form of therapy or cure for your child.

If your child is seriously depressed or if therapy is not working (and the therapist is following a reasonable course of treatment), antidepressants may be tried. This can be a scary moment for you, the parent, and justifiably so. Be sure you are confident with your physician and that you have informed yourself about medications, treatment protocols, and side effects. The World Wide Web is a wonderful source of information. Most physicians are becoming accustomed to the educated consumer.

Treatment of depression in children is usually very successful if parents willingly assist the process by making their own changes: getting their own depression treated, changing parenting styles, and increasing social supports. Successful treatment of childhood depression and continued relapse prevention mean your child has an excellent chance to live a long, healthy, and happy life. Remember from chapter 2, untreated childhood depression tends to repeat, with each successive episode being more severe. So you want to seek treatment for your child early and then practice prevention throughout his childhood in order to help avoid or catch a second episode.

## RELAX. YOU'RE DOING FINE!

Never forget that in the real world, perfection does not exist. Researchers, clinicians, and parent educators are continuously refining and changing their ideas based on the newest

## Something You Can Do #29
### *Questions to Ask Therapists and Managed Care Companies*

Therapists
- Do you have experience treating depression in children?
- What kinds of interventions do you use when treating children?
- How long are children usually in treatment with you?
- Do you include the family? If so, how?
- Are you a preferred provider or on the panel for [name your insurance or managed care company]?
- If not, do you bill insurance for out-of-network reimbursement? What is your fee?

Managed Care Companies
- What are my benefits for mental health? What are my deductibles and co-payments?
- Do you cover family therapy when the patient is a child? If so, is my co-payment the same as for individual treatment?
- Is [name therapist of your choice] on your provider panel? If not, do I have out-of-network benefits? What would be my cost?
- If no one on your panel has expertise in treating childhood depression, will you accept into your network or contract out-of-network a therapist I know who has such expertise?
- If I am not happy with the services of a therapist on your panel, can I switch therapists? What would be the procedure?

information. Parents, too, can continuously refine and change their beliefs and approaches to depression prevention as new information becomes available.

This book is not meant to be the final authority on how to reduce your child's risk for depression. In fact, I am hoping it is one of the first of many such books to be born out of yet-to-be-researched information.

When practicing the principles and activities in this book, remember to model graceful imperfection. Feel free to accept mistakes, apologize often, and try harder next time. As your children struggle to learn protective skills, use your knowledge of your own imperfections as the basis of compassion for their learning process. Most of us are slow learners, after all. This attitude, along with consistent practice, should make becoming a proactive prevention parent much more effective.

I saw the angel in the marble and carved until I set him free.

—MICHELANGELO

# NOTES

## Introduction: Becoming a Prevention Parent

1. Goodman and Gotlib, *Children of Depressed Parents,* 3.

2. Harrington et al., "Adult Outcomes of Childhood and Adolescent Depression."

3. Goodman and Gotlib, *Children of Depressed Parents,* 4.

4. Murray and Lopez, *The Global Burden of Disease.*

5. Gillham, Shatte, and Freres, "Preventing Depression."

## Chapter 1: Is Your Child at Risk for Depression?

1. Coltrera, *Understanding Depression,* 6.

2. Ibid., 7–8.

3. Ibid., 14–15.

4. Radke-Yarrow et al., *Children of Depressed Mothers.*

5. Theodore C. Dumas, "Stress and Disease: Who Gets Sick and Who Stays Well," workshop sponsored by Cortex Educational Seminars, spring 2002. Robert M. Julien, "Pharmacology of Psychotherapeutic Drugs," workshop sponsored by Northwest Psychopharmacology Seminars, spring 2002.

6. Beardslee and Gladstone, "Prevention of Childhood Depression."

7. Fassler and Dumas, *"Help Me, I'm Sad,"* 23–26. Nunley, "The Relationship of Self Esteem and Depression in Adolescence."

8. Jaycox et al., "Prevention of Depressive Symptoms in School Children."

9. Stein et al., "Social Anxiety Disorder and the Risk of Depression."

10. Cardemil, Reivich, and Seligman, "The Prevention of Depressive Symptoms in Low-Income Minority Middle School Students."

11. Yapko, *Hand Me Down Blues,* chap. 4.

## Chapter 2: What Is Childhood Depression, Really?

1. National Institute of Mental Health, "Fact Sheet."

2. National Institute of Mental Health, "Depression in Children and Adolescents."

3. Gillham, Shatte, and Freres, "Preventing Depression."

4. National Institute of Mental Health, "Fact Sheet."

5. Gillham, Shatte, and Freres, "Preventing Depression."

6. American Psychiatric Association, *Diagnostic and Statistical Manual of Mental Disorders.*

7. "Depression in Children, Part 1." "Depression in Children, Part 2."

8. Mezzacappa et al. "Tricyclic Antidepressants and Cardiac Autonomic Control in Children and Adolescents."

## Chapter 3: The Good News about Depression Prevention

1. Jaycox et al., "Prevention of Depressive Symptoms in School Children." Gillham et al., "Prevention of Depressive Symptoms in Schoolchildren: Two Year Follow-Up."

2. Yu and Seligman, "Preventing Depressive Symptoms in Chinese Children." Cardemil, Reivich, and Seligman, "The Prevention of Depressive Symptoms in Low-Income Minority Middle School Students."

3. Beardslee et al., "Examination of Children's Responses to Two Preventive Intervention Strategies Over Time."

4. Tiffany M. Field, "Prenatal Effects of Maternal Depression," in *Children of Depressed Parents: Mechanisms of Risk and Implications*

*for Treatment,* ed. Sherryl H. Goodman and Ian H. Gotlib
(Washington, D.C.: American Psychological Association, 2002),
59–88. Field, "Maternal Depression Could Last a Lifetime."
American Psychological Association, "Mirror Images." Galler
et al., "Maternal Depressive Symptoms Affect Infant Cognitive
Development in Barbados." Murray et al., "The Socioemotional
Development of 5-Year-Old Children of Postnatally Depressed
Mothers."

5. Cicchetti and Toth, "The Development of Depression in
Children and Adolescents."

## Chapter 4: How to Teach Protective Skills

1. Coloroso, *Parenting through Crisis.*

2. Zeig, *Experiencing Erickson.*

3. Zeig, *A Teaching Seminar with Milton H. Erickson, M.D.*

## Chapter 5: But Wait! What If the *Parent* Is Depressed?

1. Goodman and Gotlib, *Children of Depressed Parents,* 4.

2. "Depression in Children, Part 1."

3. Weinberg and Tronick, "Emotional Care of the At-Risk
Infant."

4. American Psychological Association, "Mirror Images."

5. Karlen Lyons-Ruth, Amy Lyubchik, Rebecca Wolfe, and
Elisa Bronfman, "Parental Depression and Child Attachment:
Hostile and Helpless Profiles of Parent and Child Behavior among
Families at Risk," in *Children of Depressed Parents: Mechanisms of Risk
and Implications for Treatment,* ed. Sherryl H. Goodman and Ian H.
Gotlib (Washington, D.C.: American Psychological Association,
2002), 89–120.

6. I use the word *parent* because, while this specific study in-
vestigated mothers, other studies are finding similar results with
fathers. The source is Modell et al., "Maternal Ratings of Child
Behavior Improve with Treatment of Maternal Depression."

## Chapter 6: Teaching Critical Thinking Skills: MIND

1. *Webster's New Collegiate Dictionary* (Springfield, Mass.: G. & C. Merriam Company, 1981).

2. Greenberger and Padesky, *Mind Over Mood.*

3. Michael D. Yapko, personal communication, April 1997.

4. Michael D. Yapko, "Hypnosis and Cognitive-Behavioral Therapy," workshop presented at the Ericksonian Approaches to Hypnosis and Psychotherapy Conference, Phoenix, Ariz., 11–14 December 1997. Critical thinking skills 3–5 were mentioned during Dr. Yapko's workshop as part of twelve "discrimination skills" to be taught to clients in therapeutic interventions. Critical thinking skills 2–5 are adapted with permission of Dr. Yapko.

5. Greenberger and Padesky, *Mind Over Mood.* The "A Situation, a Feeling, a Thought" exercise and the "A Fact, a Possibility, an Unanswerable Question" exercise are adapted with permission of Guilford Press.

## Chapter 7: Encouraging Emotional Flexibility: BODY

1. Judy Garber and Nina C. Martin, "Negative Cognitions in Offspring of Depressed Parents: Mechanisms of Risk," in *Children of Depressed Parents: Mechanisms of Risk and Implications for Treatment,* ed. Sherryl H. Goodman and Ian H. Gotlib (Washington D.C.: American Psychological Association, 2002).

2. "The ABC Theory of Emotional Disturbance and Therapy" is adapted here with the permission of Dr. Albert Ellis, Ph.D., and the Albert Ellis Institute. All rights reserved.

3. Excerpts are adapted from *The Optimistic Child,* copyright ©1995 by Martin E. P. Seligman, Ph.D., Karen Reivich, Ph.D., Lisa Jaycox, Ph.D., and Jane Gillham, Ph.D. Adapted and reprinted by permission of Houghton Mifflin Company. All rights reserved.

4. Garber and Martin, "Negative Cognitions in Offspring of Depressed Parents."

## Chapter 8: Developing Social Skills: HEART

1. Yapko, *Hand Me Down Blues,* 104–105.

2. Denton, "A Review of Literature on the Relationship between Social Skills and Academic Achievement."

3. Bandura et al., "Self-efficacy Pathways to Childhood Depression."

4. "Good Manners Let Kids Tackle Life Politely."

5. "The Spanking Debate." Goldstein and Brooks, *Raising Resilient Children,* week 1.

6. Garber and Martin, "Negative Cognitions in Offspring of Depressed Parents."

## Chapter 9: Fostering an Antidepressant Core: SOUL

1. Fassler and Dumas, *"Help Me, I'm Sad,"* 173.

2. Shell, "Let the Children Play." This excerpt is reprinted with the permission of both the author and *Hope Magazine.*

3. Fredrickson, "The Role of Positive Emotions in Positive Psychology."

4. Masters, Barden, and Ford, "Affective States, Expressive Behavior, and Learning in Children."

5. Fredrickson, "What Good Are Positive Emotions?"

6. Masters, Barden, and Ford, "Affective States, Expressive Behavior, and Learning in Children."

7. In late 2002, the U.S. Department of Education awarded Martin E. P. Seligman, Ph.D., and his team 2.8 million dollars to teach positive psychology to ninth-graders for four years in order to "learn what works." We look forward to the results.

# BIBLIOGRAPHY

American Psychiatric Association. *Diagnostic and Statistical Manual of Mental Disorders.* 4th ed. Washington, D.C.: American Psychiatric Association, 1994.

American Psychological Association. "Mirror Images: Depressed Mothers, Depressed Newborns." News release, 23 April 1997. Available on-line at www.apa.org/releases/mom.html.

Apter, A. "Four Year Follow-up of Depressed Children: Preventive Implications." *Journal of Preventive Psychiatry* 1, no. 3 (1982): 331–35.

Bandura, Albert, Concetta Pastorelli, Claudio Barbaranelli, and Gian Vittorio Caprara, "Self-efficacy Pathways to Childhood Depression." *Journal of Personality and Social Psychology* 76, no. 2 (February 1999): 258–69.

Beardslee, W. R. *Out of the Darkened Room: When a Parent Is Depressed: Protecting the Children and Strengthening the Family.* New York: Little, Brown and Company, 2002.

Beardslee, W. R., and T. R. G. Gladstone. "Prevention of Childhood Depression: Recent Findings and Future Prospects." *Biological Psychiatry* 49, no. 12 (15 June 2001): 1101–10.

Beardslee, W. R., E. J. Wright, P. Salt, K. Drezner, T. R. G. Gladstone, E. M. Versage, and P. C. Rothberg. "Examination of Children's Responses to Two Preventive Intervention Strategies Over Time." *Journal of the American Academy of Child and Adolescent Psychiatry* 36, no. 2 (February 1997): 196–204.

Beck, Judith S. *Cognitive Therapy: Basics and Beyond*. New York: Guilford Press, 1995.

Brent, D. A., D. Holder, D. Kolko, B. Birmaher, M. Baugher, C. Roth, S. Iyengar, and B. A. Johnson. "A Clinical Psychotherapy Trial for Adolescent Depression Comparing Cognitive, Family, and Supportive Therapy." *Archives of General Psychiatry* 54 (September 1997): 877–85.

Burns, J. M., G. Andrew, and M. Szabo. "Depression in Young People: What Causes It and Can We Prevent It?" *Medical Journal of Australia* 177 (7 October 2002): S93–S96.

Cardemil, E., K. J. Reivich, and M. E. P. Seligman. "The Prevention of Depressive Symptoms in Low-Income Minority Middle School Students." *Prevention and Treatment* 5 (8 May 2002). Available on-line at www.journals.apa.org/prevention.

Cicchetti, Dante, and Sheree Toth. "The Development of Depression in Children and Adolescents." *American Psychologist* 53, no. 2 (February 1998): 221–41.

Coloroso, Barbara. *Kids Are Worth It! Giving Your Child the Gift of Inner Discipline*. New York: Avon Books, 1994.

———. *Parenting through Crisis: Helping Kids in Times of Loss, Grief, and Change*. New York: HarperCollins Publishers, 2000.

Coltrera, Francesca. *Understanding Depression*. Boston: Harvard Medical School, 2001.

de Mello, Anthony. *Awakening: Conversations with the Master*. Chicago: Loyola Press, 1998.

Denton, Paula. "A Review of Literature on the Relationship between Social Skills and Academic Achievement." Northeast Foundation for Children. Available on-line at www.responsive classroom.org/_cl_feature_topic_2a.htm.

"Depression in Children, Part 1." *Harvard Mental Health Letter* 18, no. 8 (February 2002).

"Depression in Children, Part 2." *Harvard Mental Health Letter* 18, no. 9 (March 2002).

Ellen, Elizabeth Fried. "Interventions Aim to Prevent Depression in High Risk Children." *Psychiatric Times* 16, no. 9 (September 1999). Available on-line at www.psychiatrictimes.com/p990957.html.

Fassler, David G., and Lynne S. Dumas. *"Help Me, I'm Sad"*: *Recognizing, Treating, and Preventing Childhood and Adolescent Depression*. New York: Penguin Books, 1997.

Field, Tiffany. "Maternal Depression Could Last a Lifetime." *Selfhelp Magazine*. Available on-line at www.selfhelpmagazine.com/articles/parenting/matdep.html.

——. "Relative Right Frontal EEG Activation in 3 to 6 Month Old Infants of Depressed Mothers." *Developmental Psychology* 31, no. 3 (1995): 358–63.

Fredrickson, Barbara L. "The Role of Positive Emotions in Positive Psychology: The Broaden-and-Build Theory of Positive Emotions." *American Psychologist* 56, no. 3 (March 2001): 218–26.

——. "What Good Are Positive Emotions?" *Review of General Psychology* 2, no. 3 (1998): 300–319.

Freeman, Arthur. "A Psychosocial Approach for Conceptualizing Schematic Development for Cognitive Therapy." In *Cognitive Therapies in Action: An Evolving Innovative Practice*. San Francisco: Jossey-Bass Publishers, 1993.

Galler, J. R., R. Harrison, F. Ramsey, V. Forde, and S. C. Butler. "Maternal Depressive Symptoms Affect Infant Cognitive Development in Barbados." *Journal of Child Psychology and Psychiatry* 41, no. 6 (September 2000): 747–57.

Garber, J., S. Little, R. Hilsman, and K. R. Weaver. "Family Predictors of Suicidal Symptoms in Young Adolescents." *Journal of Adolescence* 21, article no. ad980161 (1998): 445–57.

Gillham, Jane E., Andrew J. Shatte, and Derek R. Freres. "Preventing Depression: A Review of Cognitive-Behavioral and Family Interventions." *Applied and Preventive Psychology* 9 (2000): 63–88.

Gillham, J. E., and K. J. Reivich. "Prevention of Depressive Symptoms in Schoolchildren: A Research Update." *Psychological Science* 10, no. 5 (September 1999): 461–62.

Gillham, J. E., K. J. Reivich, L. H. Jaycox, and M. E. P. Seligman. "Prevention of Depressive Symptoms in Schoolchildren: Two Year Follow-Up." *Psychological Science* 6, no. 6 (November 1995): 343–51.

Goldstein, Sam, and Robert Brooks. *Raising Resilient Children: A Curriculum to Foster Strength, Hope, and Optimism in Children.* Baltimore, Md.: Brookes Publishing Co., 2002.

Goleman, Daniel. *Emotional Intelligence: Why It Can Matter More Than IQ.* New York: Bantam Books, 1995.

"Good Manners Let Kids Tackle Life Politely." *Richland (Wash.) Tri-City Herald,* 19 March 2000.

Goodman, Sherryl H., and Ian H. Gotlib, eds. *Children of Depressed Parents: Mechanisms of Risk and Implications for Treatment.* Washington, D.C.: American Psychological Association, 2002.

Greenberger, D., and C. A. Padesky. *Mind Over Mood: Change How You Feel by Changing the Way You Think.* New York: Guilford Press, 1995.

Hammen, Constance, Karen Rudolph, John Weisz, Uma Rao, and Dorli Burge. "The Context of Depression in Clinic-Referred Youth: Neglected Areas in Treatment." *Journal of the American Academy of Child and Adolescent Psychiatry* 38, no. 1 (1999): 64–71.

Harrington, R., and A. Clark. "Prevention and Early Intervention for Depression in Adolescence and Early Adult Life." *European Archives of Psychiatry and Clinical Neuroscience* 248 (1998): 32–45.

Harrington, Richard, Hazel Fudge, Michael Rutter, Andrew Pickles, and Jonathan Hill. "Adult Outcomes of Childhood and

Adolescent Depression." *Archives of General Psychiatry* 47 (May 1990): 465–73.

Hockey, Kathleen P. "Primary Prevention of Childhood Depression: Beyond Biology." *Social Work Today* 2, no. 2 (21 January 2002): 9–12.

Ialongo, Nicholas S., Lisa Werthamer, Sheppard G. Kellam, C. Hendricks Brown, Songbai Wang, and Yuhua Lin. "Proximal Impact of Two First-Grade Preventive Interventions on the Early Risk Behaviors for Later Substance Abuse, Depression, and Antisocial Behavior." *American Journal of Community Psychology* 27, no. 5 (October 1999): 599–641.

Jaycox, L. H., K. J. Reivich, J. Gillham, and M. E. P. Seligman. "Prevention of Depressive Symptoms in School Children." *Behaviour Research and Therapy* 32, no. 8 (1994): 801–16.

Masters, John C., Christopher Barden, and Martin E. Ford. "Affective States, Expressive Behavior, and Learning in Children." *Journal of Personality and Social Psychology* 37, no. 3 (1979): 380–90.

McMillen, J. Curtis. "Better for It: How People Benefit from Adversity." *Social Work* 44, no. 5 (September 1999): 455–67.

Mezzacappa, Enrico, Ron Steingard, Dan Kindlon, Philip Saul, and Felton Earls. "Tricyclic Antidepressants and Cardiac Autonomic Control in Children and Adolescents." *Journal of the American Academy of Child and Adolescent Psychiatry* 37, no. 1 (1998): 52–59.

Modell, Judith D., Jack G. Modell, Jan Wallander, Bart Hodgens, Linda Duke, and Dale Wisely. "Maternal Ratings of Child Behavior Improve with Treatment of Maternal Depression." *Family Medicine* 33, no. 9 (October 2001): 691–95.

Munoz, Ricardo, and Yu-Wen Ying. *The Prevention of Depression: Research and Practice.* Baltimore, Md.: Johns Hopkins University Press, 1993.

Murray, Christopher J. L., and Alan D. Lopez, eds. *The Global*

*Burden of Disease: A Comprehensive Assessment of Mortality and Disability from Diseases, Injuries, and Risk Factors in 1990 and Projected to 2020.* Global Burden of Disease and Injury Series. Available on-line at www.who.int/msa/mnh/ems/dalys/intro.htm.

Murray, L., D. Sinclair, P. Cooper, P. Ducournau, P. Turner, and A. Stein. "The Socioemotional Development of 5-Year-Old Children of Postnatally Depressed Mothers." *Journal of Child Psychology and Psychiatry* 40, no. 8 (November 1999): 1259–71.

National Institute of Mental Health. "Depression in Children and Adolescents: A Fact Sheet for Physicians." Available on-line at www.nimh.nih.gov/publicat/depchildresfact.cfm.

————. "Fact Sheet" prepared by Depression Research at the National Institute of Mental Health. Available on-line at www.nimh.nih.gov/publicat/depresfact.cfm.

Nunley, Kathie F. "The Relationship of Self-Esteem and Depression in Adolescence." Available on-line at www.drnunley.com/depressi.htm.

Papolos, Demitri, and Janice Papolos. *The Bipolar Child: The Definitive and Reassuring Guide to Childhood's Most Misunderstood Disorder.* New York: Broadway Books, 1999.

Preston, John. *You Can Beat Depression: A Guide to Prevention and Recovery.* 3d ed. Atascadero, Calif: Impact Publishers, 2001.

Radke-Yarrow, Marian, Pedro Martinez, Anne Mayfield, and Donna Ronsaville. *Children of Depressed Mothers: From Early Childhood to Maturity.* Cambridge, United Kingdom: Cambridge University Press, 1998.

Rushton, Jerry L., Sarah J. Clark, and Gary L. Freed. "Pediatrician and Family Physician Prescription of Selective Serotonin Reuptake Inhibitors." *Pediatrics* 105, no. 6 (June 2000): e82.

Samaan, Rodney A. "The Influences of Race, Ethnicity, and Poverty on the Mental Health of Children." *Journal of Health*

*Care for the Poor and Underserved* 11, no. 1 (February 2000):
100–110.

Seligman, Martin E. P. *Authentic Happiness: Using the New Positive
Psychology to Realize Your Potential for Lasting Fulfillment.* New
York: The Free Press, 2002.

Seligman, Martin E. P., Karen Reivich, Lisa Jaycox, and Jane
Gillham. *The Optimistic Child: A Proven Program to Safeguard
Children against Depression and Build Lifelong Resilience.* Boston:
Houghton Mifflin, 1995.

Seligman, Martin E. P., Peter Schulman, Robert J. DeRubeis,
and Steven D. Hollon. "The Prevention of Depression and
Anxiety." *Prevention and Treatment* 2 (21 December 1999).
Available on-line at www.journals.apa.org/prevention.

Shatte, Andrew, Karen Reivich, Jane Gillham, and Martin E. P.
Seligman. "Learned Optimism in Children." In *Coping: The
Psychology of What Works,* edited by C. R. Snyder, 165–81. New
York: Oxford University Press, 1999.

Shell, Ellen Ruppel. "Let the Children Play." *Hope Magazine,* no. 15
(July/August 1998): 24–29.

"The Spanking Debate." *Harvard Mental Health Letter* 19, no. 5
(November 2002).

Stein, Murray B., Martina Fuetsch, Nina Muller, Michael Hofler,
Roselind Lieb, and Hans-Ulrich Wittchen. "Social Anxiety
Disorder and the Risk of Depression: A Prospective Community
Study of Adolescents and Young Adults." *Archives of General
Psychiatry* 58 (March 2001): 251–56.

Weinberg, M. Katherine, and Edward Z. Tronick. "Emotional
Care of the At-Risk Infant: Emotional Characteristics of
Infants Associated with Maternal Depression and Anxiety."
*Pediatrics* 102, no. 5, supplement (November 1998):
1298–1304.

Weissman, M. M., V. Warner, P. Wickramaratne, D. Moreau, and

M. Olfson. "Offspring of Depressed Parents: 10 Years Later."
*Archives of General Psychiatry* 54 (October 1997): 932–40.

Witkin, Georgia. "Kid Stress." *USA Weekend,* 5–7 February 1999, 18.

Wylie, Mary Sykes, and Richard Simon. "Discoveries from the
Black Box: How the Neuro-Science Revolution Can Change
Your Practice." *Psychotherapy Networker* 26, no. 5 (September/
October 2002): 26–37, 68.

Yapko, Michael D. *Breaking the Patterns of Depression.* New York:
Doubleday, 1997.

———. *Hand Me Down Blues: How to Stop Depression from Spreading
in Families.* New York: Golden Books, 1999.

Yu, David Lei, and Martin E. P. Seligman. "Preventing Depressive
Symptoms in Chinese Children." *Prevention and Treatment* 5
(8 May 2002). Available on-line at www.journals.apa.org/
prevention.

Zeig, Jeffrey. *A Teaching Seminar with Milton H. Erickson, M.D.* New
York: Brunner-Routledge, 1980.

———. *Experiencing Erickson: An Introduction to the Man and His
Work.* New York: Brunner/Mazel, 1985.

# RESOURCES

The Academy of Cognitive Therapy
610-664-1273
www.academyofct.org

American Association for Marriage and Family Therapy
112 South Alfred Street
Alexandria, VA 22314-3061
703-838-9808
www.aamft.org

American Psychiatric Association
1000 Wilson Boulevard, Suite 1825
Arlington, VA 22209-3901
703-907-7300
www.psych.org

American Psychological Association
750 First Street Northeast
Washington, DC 20002-4242
800-374-2721
www.apa.org

National Association of Social Workers
750 First Street Northeast, Suite 700
Washington, DC 20002-4241
202-408-8600
www.naswdc.org

University of Pennsylvania Health System
Department of Psychiatry
Center for Cognitive Therapy
Referral List by State
www.uphs.upenn.edu/psycct/referral/states.htm

## GENERAL RESOURCES

Albert Ellis Institute
45 East 65th Street
New York, NY 10021
800-323-4738
www.rebt.org

American Academy of Child and Adolescent Psychiatry
3615 Wisconsin Avenue Northwest
Washington, DC 20016-3007
202-966-7300
www.aacap.org

American Academy of Pediatrics
141 Northwest Point Boulevard
Elk Grove Village, IL 60007-1098
847-434-4000
www.aap.org

Depression Awareness, Recognition, and Treatment (D/ART)
5600 Fishers Lane, Room 10-85
Rockville, MD 20857
800-421-4211

The Martin Seligman Research Alliance
University of Pennsylvania
Department of Psychology
3815 Walnut Street
Philadelphia, PA 19104-6196
215-898-7173
www.positivepsychology.org

Mental Health Advancement Resource Center
Independence Square
500 Prospect Street
Pawtucket, RI 02860
401-726-8383
www.mharc.org

National Alliance for the Mentally Ill
Colonial Place Three
2107 Wilson Boulevard, Suite 300
Arlington, VA 22201
703-524-7600
NAMI Helpline: 800-950-NAMI (800-950-6264)
www.nami.org

National Mental Health Association
2001 North Beauregard Street, Twelfth Floor
Alexandria, VA 22311
703-684-7722
Mental Health Resource Center: 800-969-NMHA (800-969-
6642)
www.nmha.org

Office of Special Education Programs
Office of Special Education and Rehabilitative Services
U.S. Department of Education
400 Maryland Avenue Southwest
Washington, DC 20202
202-205-5507
www.ed.gov/offices/OSERS/OSEP/index.html

SELF-HELP BOOKS LISTED BY CATEGORY

## Childhood Depression and Treatment

Dubuque, Nicholas, and Susan E. Dubuque. *Kid Power Tactics for Dealing with Depression*. King of Prussia, Pa.: The Center for Applied Psychology, Inc., 1996.

Fassler, David G., and Lynne S. Dumas. *"Help Me, I'm Sad": Recognizing, Treating, and Preventing Childhood and Adolescent Depression*. New York: Penguin Books, 1997.

Lynn, George T. *Survival Strategies for Parenting Children with Bipolar Disorder*. London: Jessica Kingsley Publications, 2000.

Miller, Jeffrey. *The Childhood Depression Sourcebook*. New York: Contemporary Books, 1999.

Papolos, Demitri, and Janice Papolos. *The Bipolar Child: The Definitive and Reassuring Guide to Childhood's Most Misunderstood Disorder*. New York: Broadway Books, 1999.

Riley, Douglas A. *The Depressed Child: A Parent's Guide for Rescuing Kids*. Dallas, Tex.: Taylor Trade Publishing, 2000.

Seligman, Martin E. P., Karen Reivich, Lisa Jaycox, and Jane Gillham. *The Optimistic Child: A Proven Program to Safeguard Children against Depression and Build Lifelong Resilience*. Boston: Houghton Mifflin, 1995.

Shaffer, David, and Bruce Wastick. *Many Faces of Depression in Children and Adolescents*. Washington, D.C.: American Psychiatric Press, 2002.

Yapko, Michael D. *Hand Me Down Blues: How to Stop Depression from Spreading in Families*. New York: Golden Books, 1999.

## Adult Depression and Treatment

Beardslee, W. R. *Out of the Darkened Room: When a Parent Is Depressed: Protecting the Children and Strengthening the Family*. New York: Little, Brown and Company, 2002.

Clark, Lynn. *SOS Help for Emotions: Managing Anxiety, Anger, and Depression*. Bowling Green, Ky.: Parent's Press, 1998.

Coltrera, Francesca. *Understanding Depression*. Boston: Harvard Medical School, 2001.

Greenberger, D., and C. A. Padesky. *Mind Over Mood: Change How You Feel by Changing the Way You Think*. New York: Guilford Press, 1995.

Nicholson, Joanne, Alexis D. Henry, Jonathan C. Clayfield, and Susan M. Phillips. *Parenting Well When You're Depressed: A Complete Resource for Maintaining a Healthy Family*. Oakland, Calif.: New Harbinger Publications, Inc., 2001.

O'Conner, Richard. *Undoing Depression: What Therapy Doesn't Teach You and Medication Can't Give You*. New York: Little, Brown and Company, 1997.

Preston, John. *You Can Beat Depression: A Guide to Prevention and Recovery*. 3d ed. Atascadero, Calif.: Impact Publishers, 2001.

Yapko, Michael D. *Breaking the Patterns of Depression.* New York:
    Doubleday, 1997.


## Parenting and Resiliency

Brooks, Robert, and Sam Goldstein. *Raising Resilient Children:
    Fostering Strength, Hope, and Optimism in Your Child.* Chicago, Ill.:
    Contemporary Books, 2001.

Coloroso, Barbara. *Kids Are Worth It! Giving Your Child the Gift of
    Inner Discipline.* New York: Avon Books, 1994.

————. *Parenting through Crisis: Helping Kids in Times of Loss, Grief,
    and Change.* New York: HarperCollins Publishers, 2000.

Gottman, John. *Raising an Emotionally Intelligent Child: The Heart of
    Parenting.* New York: Simon and Schuster, 1997.

*Parenting for Prevention Information Series, The.* Center City, Minn.:
    Hazelden, 1998.

Reivich, Karen, and Andrew Shatte. *The Resilience Factor: How
    Changing the Way You Think Will Change Your Life for the Good: 7
    Essential Skills for Overcoming Life's Inevitable Obstacles.* New York:
    Broadway Books, 2002.

Roehikepartain, Jolene, and Nancy Leffert. *What Young Children
    Need to Succeed.* Minneapolis, Minn.: Free Spirit Publishing,
    Inc., 2000.

Seligman, Martin E. P. *Authentic Happiness: Using the New Positive
    Psychology to Realize Your Potential for Lasting Fulfillment.* New
    York: The Free Press, 2002.

Shapiro, Lawrence E. *An Ounce of Prevention: How Parents Can Stop
    Childhood Behavioral and Emotional Problems before They Start.*
    New York: HarperCollins Publishers, 2000.

————. *How to Raise a Child with a High EQ: A Parents' Guide to
    Emotional Intelligence.* New York: HarperCollins Publishers,
    1997.

## Biology and the Brain

Amen, Daniel G. *Healing the Hardware of the Soul: How Making the Brain-Soul Connection Can Optimize Your Life, Love, and Spiritual Growth.* New York: Free Press, 2002.

Goleman, Daniel. *Emotional Intelligence: Why It Can Matter More Than IQ.* New York: Bantam Books, 1995.

Ledoux, Joseph. *The Emotional Brain: The Mysterious Underpinnings of Emotional Life.* New York: Simon and Schuster, 1996.

Siegel, Daniel. *The Developing Mind: How Relationships and the Brain Interact to Shape Who We Are.* New York: Guilford Press, 1999.

## Critical Thinking Skills

Shure, Myrna B., and Roberta Israeloff. *Raising a Thinking Pre-teen: The "I Can Problem-Solve" Program for 8–12 Year Olds.* New York: Henry Holt and Company, 2000.

Shure, Myrna B., Theresa Fay Digeronimo, and Jackie Aher. *Raising a Thinking Child Workbook: Teaching Young Children How to Resolve Everyday Conflicts and Get Along with Others.* Champaign, Ill.: Research Press, 2000.

## Social Skills

Cohen, Cathi. *Raise Your Child's Social IQ: Stepping Stones to People Skills for Kids.* Silver Spring, Md.: Advantage Books, 2000.

Frankel, Fred. *Good Friends Are Hard to Find: Help Your Child Find, Make, and Keep Friends.* Glendale, Calif.: Perspective Publishing, 1996.

Fraser, M., J. Nash, M. Galinsky, and K. Darwin. *Making Choices: Social Problem-Solving Skills for Children.* Washington D.C.: The NASW Press, 2000.

# INDEX

ABC Theory of Emotional
Disturbance and Therapy,
122–23
adjustment disorder with
depressed mood, 29
adult depression, 69, 70
See also clinical depression
building personal awareness
of, 80–81
causes of, 78, 81–82, 178
diagnosing, 26–27
effects on children, 2–3,
22, 67, 68, 69, 70, 122
linked to childhood
depression, 2
needs-fulfillment and, 173
negative beliefs and, 74–75,
122
recovering from, 89–90
relapses of, 91–93
self-defeating thoughts and,
68, 70
treatment for. See treatment
of depression
adversity training, 48–51
learning from role models,
63, 64

problem-solving techniques
as, 60
American Academy of Child
and Adolescent Psychiatry,
35
American Academy of
Pediatrics (AAP), 19, 20
antidepressants, 13, 35, 83, 84,
172
for children, 35, 182
anxiety disorders, 16–17
assertiveness, 144–47

Beardslee, William R., 3, 41
Beck, Judith, 4
belief systems, 87–89
See also core beliefs
contributing to childhood
depression, 125–26, 128
negative, 74–75, 122
biology of depression, 12–15
Bipolar Child, The (Papolos/
Papolos), 28–29
bipolar depression, 28–29, 67
brain chemistry, 13, 15, 25,
172–73
Busch, Bernie, 72

# INDEX OF "SOMETHING" ACTIVITIES

# ABOUT THE AUTHOR

Kathleen Panula Hockey is a licensed clinical social worker in private practice in Richland, Washington, where she resides with her husband and two children. She is also a recognized speaker on the topic of preventing childhood depression. You can visit her at www.depressionfreechildren.com.

**Hazelden Publishing and Educational Services** is a division of the Hazelden Foundation, a not-for-profit organization. Since 1949, Hazelden has been a leader in promoting the dignity and treatment of people afflicted with the disease of chemical dependency.

The mission of the foundation is to improve the quality of life for individuals, families, and communities by providing a national continuum of information, education, and recovery services that are widely accessible; to advance the field through research and training; and to improve our quality and effectiveness through continuous improvement and innovation.

Stemming from that, the mission of this division is to provide quality information and support to people wherever they may be in their personal journey—from education and early intervention, through treatment and recovery, to personal and spiritual growth.

Although our treatment programs do not necessarily use everything Hazelden publishes, our bibliotherapeutic materials support our mission and the Twelve Step philosophy upon which it is based. We encourage your comments and feedback.

The headquarters of the Hazelden Foundation are in Center City, Minnesota. Additional treatment facilities are located in Chicago, Illinois; Newberg, Oregon; New York, New York; Plymouth, Minnesota; St. Paul, Minnesota; and West Palm Beach, Florida. At these sites, we provide a continuum of care for men and women of all ages. Our Plymouth facility is designed specifically for youth and families.

For more information on Hazelden, please call 1-800-257-7800. Or you may access our World Wide Web site on the Internet at www.hazelden.org.